DEFYING CONVENTION
WOMEN WHO CHANGED THE RULES

WOMEN
WRITERS

PAULA JOHANSON

Enslow Publishing
101 W. 23rd Street
Suite 240
New York, NY 10011
USA

enslow.com

"The memory of my mother has always been the pride and delight of my life."

— Mary Shelley

And for Alyx and Kellyoyo, dancing at the British Museum

Published in 2017 by Enslow Publishing, LLC.
101 W. 23rd Street, Suite 240, New York, NY 10011

Library of Congress Cataloging-in-Publication Data

Names: Johanson, Paula, author.
Title: Women writers / Paula Johanson.
Description: New York, NY : Enslow Publishing, 2017. | Series: Defying convention : women who changed the rules | Includes bibliographical references and index.
Identifiers: LCCN 2016021454 | ISBN 9780766081451 (library bound)
Subjects: LCSH: Women authors—Biography—Juvenile literature.
Classification: LCC PN471 .J64 2016 | DDC 809/.89287—dc23
LC record available at https://lccn.loc.gov/2016021454

Printed in Malaysia

To Our Readers: We have done our best to make sure all websites in this book were active and appropriate when we went to press. However, the author and the publisher have no control over and assume no liability for the material available on those websites or on any websites they may link to. Any comments or suggestions can be sent by e-mail to customerservice@enslow .com.

CONTENTS

Women have been writing since the beginning of time. As modern humans spread from Africa into other continents, they carved symbols onto cave walls around the world.[1] Some marks are only a dot, or a wavy line, or a handprint, and many of these handprints are the size and shape of women's hands.

In ancient days, writing reflected that both men and women were important to their cultures, but since then, cultures have changed and the writing of women marginalized. In many cultures, men were considered superior to women. Formal education in reading and writing was often reserved for men. In many cultures, women were educated only enough to make them able to maintain their homes. Writing for a wide audience was usually done by men.

Though history is dominated by male writers writing about men, female writers are gradually being recognized as the participants they were in recording our human history.

When authorities set out to control a woman writer, they usually began by condemning her sexuality rather than discussing her topics or how well she wrote; she was usually called a harlot, or a sexless freak, or

Women have been recording their experiences and expressing their imaginations through the written word for centuries. But for many years, writing was considered the domain of men.

both. Women were held to a different standard of conduct from men. "Man is defined as a human being, and a woman as female," wrote Simone de Beauvoir. "Whenever she behaves as a human being, she is said to imitate the male."[2]

CHAPTER ONE

WOMEN WRITING BEFORE THE CHRISTIAN ERA

Writing was a tool of civilization for cultures near the Mediterranean Sea for some two thousand years before the Christian Church was formed. As time went on, writing became their formal way to record history. Other cultures in Africa continued to rely on a *griot's* recitations of family histories or a *jeli's* poetry about events; and in northern Europe people depended on the oral memory of a bard or the chanting of a *scop*, but the cultures that relied on writing made formal records of their history.

Among written history preserved from the time of Ancient Greece to the emergence of the Christian church, the consistent point of view was that of men writing about the actions of men. What women did and what they wrote about were generally not considered history to be recorded. This chapter discusses a sample of women writers who were exceptions to this trend, from before the time of Christianity, as a powerful cultural agency.

MAKEDA (CA. 960–910 BCE)

In Ethiopia, Makeda was the ruler described in the Bible as the Queen of Sheba. She was born about the year 960 BCE. Presentations of her in both the Old Testament and New Testament vary from how she is described in the Quran and in

The writings of Makeda, also known as the Queen of Sheba, were not preserved.

Ethiopian writings.[1] Her name is not recorded in the Bible, but in Muslim writing it is said to be Bilqis. The name Makeda might be a version of a word in that part of the world for "ruling queen." Oral traditions in African history have surrounded this ruler with a variety of legends, much as oral traditions in Britain built up around King Arthur. These traditions were recorded in the Ethiopian book *Kebra Nagast* (Glory of the Kings), a fourteenth-century CE compilation of regional oral histories.[2]

Sheba is a land identified as Saba, a part of Arabia close to Ethiopia. Land on both sides of this narrow part of the Red Sea was formerly ruled as one country. The king and queen had passed their throne to their son, and at his death the heir was their daughter, Makeda. A confident ruler,

Makeda was wealthy, powerful, and witty. She was educated in the skills necessary to lead and manage her country, and wrote on alchemy, the science that was the forerunner of modern chemistry. Descriptions of her appearance vary widely, even as to the color of her skin and hair, but the stories agree she was very attractive and knowledgeable. Some Biblical scholars consider her to be the woman protagonist in the Song of Songs, who says "I am black, but comely."[3]

Upon learning of King Solomon of the Jews, this intelligent and powerful reigning queen traveled from her homeland to Jerusalem. Having heard of his reputation for wisdom, she wished to see if the rumors were true. Her intelligence and knowledge were apparent while she questioned him closely. Satisfied that he was a wise man, she gave him great gifts, including camels loaded with wonderful spices as well as the gifts the Magi would bring later to Christ: gold, myrrh, and frankincense. Some Jewish scholars report that the alchemists, to test his wisdom, said one of her gifts was the philosopher's stone, but Solomon already knew the secret and recognized the stone on sight.[4]

Did they fall in love or did Solomon trick her? The stories vary, but together Makeda and Solomon conceived a son who was named Menalik. Though invited to stay in Jerusalem as the king's wife, Makeda returned home with her son. Solomon already had seven hundred wives, and Makeda was unwilling to stay. She returned to Ethiopia and continued her rule there as the mother of a royal family. Her line of descendants became Ethiopian kings for the next two thousand years. Among the descendants of her son Menalik the First are the Ethiopian Jews, who since about 400 CE have called themselves Beta Israel (House of Israel), and Bene Israel for those who converted to Christianity. Recent genetic studies confirm Jewish ancestry for these Ethiopians.[5]

Makeda made profound impressions on the Middle East and Mediterranean world with her talents, wise writings, and security as a leader who dared travel on this adventure.[6] These impressions were later recorded by the church writers Josephus and Origen, and by her image in art of the time. Her power as a leader was undisputed by church writers, who noted her physical charm, beauty, and wisdom yet did not preserve her writings along with the proverbs written by Solomon.[7] It seems to some scholars that while the report of her state visit to Jerusalem was a fact that could not in good conscience be suppressed, her words of wisdom were edited out of the books that later became the Bible. The lingering reputation of the Queen of Sheba for many readers is an impression of a beautiful woman swanning her way through a meeting with a powerful king, rather than an influential monarch making a visit of state.

SAPPHO (CA. 630–580 BCE)

In classical Greek times, Sappho was an honored poet. Sappho was born about the year 630 BCE into a family of aristocrats in the town of Mytilene on the island of Lesbos; this Greek island is near the ruins of Troy in what is now modern Turkey. She had at least two brothers and dedicated a poem to one of them, a fragment of which has survived to the present day. As a young woman, she married a successful merchant. Together they had a daughter named Cleis, named for Sappho's mother. She apparently lived past middle age, as in at least one poem she mentions her formerly brown hair going gray and complains of pains in her knees.

With the leisure brought by wealth, she chose to spend her time studying the arts on the island of Lesbos, which was a cultural center. She traveled throughout Greece as well. Political activities in her family led to her exile for a time, which she spent in Sicily. The residents of Syracuse were honored to have this celebrated poet visit, and they commemorated her stay by erecting a statue to her.

Her works were known as melê (songs). The poetry Sappho wrote was intended to be accompanied by the playing of a lyre (a kind of harp), so it is called lyrical poetry, and she was a lyrist. The influence of such poetry has come down to modern English, so that the words for songs are called lyrics.

For lyric poetry, Sappho created innovations in both technique and style. She refined the lyric meter to what is now called Sapphic meter. As part of a new wave of lyricists, she changed the focus from writing from the point of view of gods and inspiring Muses, to writing from a personal point of view. Her poems are among the first to speak of love and loss from personal experience. Her sensual and melodic style

Greek writer Sappho was considered the female counterpart to Homer. He was known as "the Poet" and she as "the Poetess."

led her to write love songs of yearning and reflection. She also invented a new style of lyre as well as the plectrum, which is a small flexible piece of bone or tortoiseshell used to pluck the strings. Modern guitarists call it a pick.

In her poetry, the object of her affections was usually female, often one of the many women students who came to her to be educated in the arts. Sappho taught and supported these students and wrote them poems of adoration. When they left the island to be married, she composed their wedding songs. Because the homoerotic element of her poetry was not suppressed in Ancient Greece, it seems that female homosexuality was not condemned at that time. Later scholars, particularly during the nineteenth century CE, dismissed her work. Sappho has become so linked to love between women that two of the words for female homosexuality—sapphic and lesbian—are derived from study of her poetry.

Plato elevated Sappho to the status of a Muse, one of the daughters of the god Apollo, whose duties were to inspire artists. He also referred to her as beautiful, though a later writer insisted she was short and swarthy with brown hair and skin, unlike the Greek ideal of pale skin for women. People whose hair was not black or golden would dye their hair if they could afford to. In classic Greece, raunchy jokes were told about people from Lesbos, and about Sappho being a girl from that time and place. Dirty jokes of that kind about public figures were common, even in plays by Aristophanes and other celebrated writers.

The scientist and writer Aristotle reported that Sappho was honored, despite her gender. According critic Daniel Mendelson, "many scholars now see her poetry as an attempt to appropriate and 'feminize' the diction and subject matter of heroic epic."[8] One of her poems called on the goddess of love, Aphrodite, to be her aid in writing about love—an interesting parallel to the beginning of Homer's epic poem *The Iliad*, in which he called on Calliope, the Muse of epic poetry, to aid him in writing of the rage of Achilles. On hearing one of Sappho's songs performed by a neighbor, the Athenian leader Solon, who was both a lawyer and a poet, asked to be taught the song, "Because I want to learn it and die."⁹

There is a legend that Sappho leapt from a cliff to certain death in the sea, because of unrequited love for Phaon, a younger man who was a sailor. Four hundred years after her death, the Library at Alexandria recorded nine volumes of Sappho's poetry preserved. The Library honored her in their canon of nine lyric geniuses. Time has taken its toll on those poems through neglect, fire, and flood—and perhaps censorship. Only one entire poem is preserved, along with several fragments quoted in the works of later Greek and Roman writers. Late in the nineteenth century in the Nile Valley, papyrus that had been used to wrap mummies was investigated and it was found to illustrate writings from the first to tenth century CE. Among these papyrus strips were parts of a few more poems by Sappho, which were copied by a monk. These scraps are all of the preserved work of Sappho that exists. A few other papyrus finds have recently been discovered and are still being investigated.

ASPASIA (CA. 470–410 BCE)

In Athens, Greece, Aspasia of Miletus was a teacher, writer, and intellectual, something very rare for a woman in the male-dominated societies of the eastern Mediterranean shores. Around the year 470

Aspasia of Miletus is regarded as a great intellectual and educator of ancient Greece.

BCE, Aspasia was born in the Ionian Greek colony of Miletus in Asia Minor (known as Turkey in the present day). It is likely that her family of birth was wealthy, because she is known to have been highly educated. She arrived in Athens in about 450 BCE to live there as a *metic*, or resident alien, since only men born in Athens were citizens. Scholars debate over how or why she traveled there. Some sources say that her older sister married the statesman and general Alcibiades during the time he was ostracized from Athens; after spending his expulsion in Miletus, Alcibiades returned to Athens and brought home not only his wife but also young Aspasia.

As a young woman, Aspasia may have "spent some time as a *hetaera*, a sort of concubine, companion, or even a prostitute."[10] It is possible that Aspasia may have been the name given to her or chosen by her rather than her birth name, as it means "welcome" or "greeting with affection."

Around 445 BCE, she operated a salon, and her beauty and intellect brought her to the attention of

Pericles, a relative of Alcibiades, who had recently divorced his first wife. Aspasia and Pericles became lovers. Apart from that fact, modern readers must realize that everything else written about Aspasia, by ancient writers from Plato to Plutarch, is based on their own biases.

Aspasia had not been born in Athens, so she could not legally marry Pericles—ironically, under a law that he had passed shortly before her arrival in the city-state. Women in Athens were either slaves or wives and considered the property of a man who was a citizen noble. Wives were secluded within their households, and home tutored only in the skills to manage the home, primarily sewing, weaving, and perhaps dance or playing the flute. But a foreigner like Aspasia was free from that legal restraint. She began to manage her own household and paid taxes. She became educated in literature and science and met socially with men and women; therefore, she was outside the social standards of Athenians.

Her influence on Pericles as an administrator was threatening to some Athenians, who targeted both of them with scandalous rumors and personal attacks, calling Aspasia a whore and the mother of Pericles's bastard. Prostitution was legal in Athens if the prostitute was not a citizen. Athenaeus, a third-century grammarian, claimed that Pericles squandered much of his property on Aspasia. Plutarch wrote that Pericles kissed her every day, both when he left the house and when he returned. Meanwhile, other Athenian citizens brought their wives to Aspasia to be educated in conversation and the intellect. Whether her home in Athens was a salon for intellectuals, a renowned school for girls, or a brothel depends on who was writing about Aspasia.

She was a complex woman who seems to have had all of the virtues and defects attributed to her. Considered clever with words, Aspasia wrote the great speeches given by Pericles as a statesman, orator, and general. Their son became another great Athenian general, also named Pericles. She taught Socrates strategies for argument, and modeled them for him in dialogues and discussion; he deferred to her greater knowledge in household management and in the economic partnership between spouses. The historian Xenophon, the orator Cicero, and the teacher Plato all admired her rhetoric, philosophy, and opinions on current events. On one occasion, Aspasia was charged with impiety, but Pericles spoke in her defense at her trial, and so she was saved from the death penalty.

A great plague struck Athens in 430 BCE, later identified as *Variola minor*, a form of smallpox. As both of Pericles's sons by his first wife died in the plague, he petitioned the court to name his son by Aspasia to be a citizen and his heir. After the death of Pericles in 429 BCE, Aspasia lived with Lysicles as her patron, and was a great help to this general

with his political career. She died around the year
410 BCE, a few years before her son. "In classical
literature, there are witty hetairai and ones of
divine beauty, those who are generous with wealth
and others who destroyed it," wrote one scholar.
"Whatever power they had came from their ability
to be recognized by the powerful men with whom
they consorted, who would love them and made
them their mistresses or concubines."[11]

Although many of her contemporaries wrote
about Aspasia, her writings are preserved only in
quotations by other writers. Since the nineteenth
and twentieth centuries CE, Aspasia has been recognized as a teacher of great ability and intellect.
"When we need Aspasia to be a chaste muse and
teacher, she is there; when we need a grand hori-
zontal, she is there, when we need a proto-feminist,
she is there also," wrote Madeleine Henry.[12] In 2007,
the award-winning author Dave Duncan needed a
name for a character in his historical fantasy novel,
one who was both politically astute and a courtesan
of upper-class Venice; there was no better choice for
her name than Aspasia.

HYPATIA (CA. 370–415)

The first woman recorded to make great contribution to mathematics, Hypatia became head of the
Neoplatonic school at Alexandria in Egypt. Hypatia

was born about the year 370 CE in Alexandria, a city as troubled with civil unrest then as Baghdad or Beirut are today. She was daughter to Theon of Alexandria. Nothing is known about Hypatia's mother, but that is not unusual for this era. What is unusual is how much education this young girl received, and how successful she became in public life and as an academic.

Intent on producing a perfect human being, Theon set high standards for his daughter. He trained her in the arts, literature, philosophy, and science. But he was not only her intellect he . He insisted that she be physically active as well. To become physically fit, she learned to handle boats, to swim, and to ride horses. Hypatia was also given speech training to enhance her abilities as an orator and a lecturer. As a young adult, she traveled to Athens, attending a school where she earned fame as a mathematician.

On her return to Alexandria, the institute where her father taught requested that Hypatia become a teacher there in both mathematics and astronomy. She lectured on Diophantus, a prominent mathematician, discussing his techniques, solutions to the problems he set, and his symbolism. She lectured as well on Plato, Plotinus, and Aristotle. Her students included pagans, Christians, and foreign scholars, who traveled from all over the known world to hear Hypatia teach. At about 400 CE, she became head of the Platonist school at Alexandria.

As well as her lecture notes, Hypatia wrote

many treatises. Most of her works were textbooks for helping her students learn difficult concepts in mathematics. Among her works were her analysis of her father's commentary on *Elements* by Euclid, and commentaries on *The Conics* by Apollonius, and *Amagest*, in which Ptolemy's many star observations were recorded. It's not known how many treatises she wrote or coedited with her father, because most were destroyed in centuries to come when libraries were purged of pagan authors by Christians. During her own lifetime, Hypatia would have seen the destruction of the temple of Serapis by order of the emperor Theodosius the first, and libraries that may have been the remnants of the fabled Library of Alexandria.[13]

Synesius of Cyrene was her most famous pupil, before he became the Bishop of Ptolemais in 410. Much of what is known about Hypatia comes from their letters. In their correspondence, Synesius gives Hypatia credit for inventing an improved astrolabe and a planisphere, instruments for studying the stars. He also acknowledged the instruments she created to distill water, to measure its level, and for determining the specific gravity of a liquid. Rather than inventing the original instruments, Hypatia probably devised improvements to existing models.

All of Hypatia's contemporary commentators describe her as a charismatic teacher of Platonic philosophy, but two hundred years later John of

Nikiu, an Egyptian Coptic bishop, wrote that she was a Hellenistic pagan, devoted to magic, astrolabes, and musical instruments, beguiling people with her Satanic wiles. He did not speak for all Christians or for all Church scholars, some of whom then and in centuries to come considered Hypatia to be a model of virtue. A Christian historian of the time praised her "extraordinary dignity and virtue"[14] when speaking before the city's magistrates. Michael Deakin wrote in his 2007 book *Hypatia of Alexandria*: "Almost alone, virtually the last academic, she stood for intellectual values, for rigorous mathematics, ascetic Neoplatonism, the crucial role of the mind, and the voice of temperance and moderation in civic life."[15]

As a Neoplatonic philosopher, Hypatia belonged to a school of Greek thought, which held different beliefs from some of the Christian church leaders of the time. Platonists and Neoplatonists were considered heretics by some church leaders. Other Christian thinkers and leaders were themselves Neoplatonists. It has been suggested that the origin of the story of Saint Catherine was based on Hypatia.[16]

When Cyril became the patriarch of the church in Egypt in 412, he promoted the belief that social unrest caused by disagreements between himself and Orestes, the prefect of Egypt, was the result of Hypatia's friendship with Orestes. In March 415,

Cyril convinced a group of religious fanatics that the way to bring peace back to Alexandria was through the death of Hypatia. At his urging, the mob pulled Hypatia from her chariot on her way to the university. They stripped her and dragged her to the

The renowned intellectual Hypatia was dragged from her chariot and murdered at the insistence of church patriarch Cyril.

church at Caesarion, where she was butchered with broken tiles. The pieces of her body were taken to Cinaron and burned.

No one was condemned for the murder of Hypatia, not the Christian fanatics or Cyril nor the church, wrote the historian Socrates Scholasticus, who lamented, "And surely nothing can be farther from the spirit of Christianity than the allowance of massacres, fights, and transactions of that sort."[17]

After her murder, many scholars departed Alexandria, marking the beginning of the decline of Alexandria as a major center of learning. The publisher of a 2007 biography of Hypatia declared that "this outrageous crime has made Hypatia a powerful symbol of intellectual freedom and feminist aspiration to this day."[18]

CHAPTER TWO

WOMEN WRITERS IN THE MIDDLE AGES

After the fall of the Roman Empire, the Mediterranean area endured a thousand years of lost technology, as well as unstable governments and economies. Scholarship was preserved in isolated Christian monasteries and later flourished in Islamic centers. The great civilizations of China and India continued with far easier transitions between dynasties. Literacy was not a skill of the common people, particularly in women; women writers were rare.

In many cultures during the Middle Ages, women were not full citizens, having instead the status of a child or an idiot as a legal infant—someone who can't put words together properly. This chapter discusses a sample of women writers from the time between the Roman Empire and the modern world.

AISHA (613 OR 614–678)

The most controversial of the Prophet Muhammad's wives, Aisha had an active role in the founding years of Islam. Born around 614 CE in Mecca, Arabia, Aisha bint Abi Bakr's mother was Umm Ruman, a respected woman of great beauty and a distant relative of Muhammad. Aisha's father was Abu Bakr, a successful businessman, who was one of the first converts to the new faith. There are many ways to spell her name in various languages.

Aisha was an important figure in the history of Islam, along with Muhammad's first wife, Khadija, and their daughter Fatima. Muhammad had married wives in part to give him family ties that would help him to succeed, but he cared for them deeply. Before the marriage of Muhammad and Aisha, Muhammad had been married for twenty-five years to

Aisha was married to the Prophet Muhammad and had great influence over the development of Islam after his death.

The date of her death is not precisely known; it is probably after 1155. Considered China's greatest woman poet during her lifetime, Li Qingzhao is still as highly regarded today as a master of *wanyue pai* (the delicate restraint). Only around a hundred of her poems have survived. In a striking tribute, astronomers have named two impact craters after Li, one on the planet Mercury and the other on the planet Venus.

HILDEGARD OF BINGEN (1098–1179)

Long venerated as a saint, Hildegard's discovery and promotion by feminists has led to much study of her life. Born in Bemersheim, West Franconia, (now part of Germany) in 1098, Hildegard was the tenth child of a prosperous knight. At eight years old, her parents brought her to be educated in a convent, newly added to a four hundred-year-old Benedictine monastery, Mount Saint Disibode. Calling Hildegard their family tithe to God, her parents put her into the care of Jutta, a noblewoman resident there, who taught the child to read and write.

When Jutta became abbess, other young noble-women were attracted to the convent. Together they learned Latin, read scriptures, and had access to many books of religion and philosophy. At eighteen,

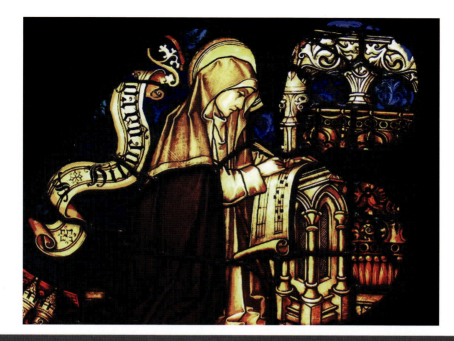

Hildegard of Bingen was a nun known for her accomplishments as a writer. She wrote music, poetry, scientific texts, and commentary, as well as letters to important world leaders.

Hildegard took her vows. Part of the Benedictine rule is labor, and Hildegard worked there as a nurse; she also copied manuscripts.

At Jutta's death, Hildegard was chosen by her fellow nuns to be their superior. When ordered by her confessor to write down the visions she had been seeing since childhood, Hildegard took ten years to write her first book. Pope Eugenius III sent a commission to inquire into her writing. The commission found her teaching orthodox and her insights authentic. He reported this to the Pope, who sent her a letter approving her continued work. In her reply, she urged the Pope to work harder for reform of the Church. During this time, Benedictine monks and nuns were encouraged to concentrate on the inner experience, personal meditation, an immediate relationship with God, and visions. But there was strife between papal authority and the authority of the Holy Roman emperor.

Her growing community of nuns did not have adequate room. Hildegard moved her abbey to a location near Bingen, completely independently, and supervised construction of their building. The abbot they had left opposed their departure, and the resulting tensions took a long time to heal.[6]

Hildegard of Bingen wrote over three hundred letters to people who wanted her advice or prayers. Her correspondents included St. Bernard of Clairvaux, and King Henry II of England and his wife, Eleanor of Aquitaine. She wrote letters advising both the German Emperor Frederick Barbarossa and the archbishop of Main. Some seventy of her poems, much of her music, and nine books have been preserved. Two of her books discuss herbal medicine, gynecology, and physiology. She wrote commentaries as well on the Gospels and the Athanasian Creed. For her, as for many medieval writers, theology, medicine, music, and similar topics were interconnected, not separate spheres of knowledge.

Some feminists have maintained that Hildegard, while a model of an educated woman active in the public sphere, was not a feminist in the modern sense. She celebrated her community of women and their worthy actions. She advocated a more conservative theology of the church, and she wrote of women in very traditional terms, even though she went beyond that tradition herself. She traveled in Germany and managed her abbey, independent of a pastor.

Hildegard was not canonized by the Roman Catholic Church as a saint until 2012. Pope Benedict XVI also named her as a Doctor of the Church, meaning that her teachings are recommended doctrine. She was the fourth woman to be so honored, after Teresa of Avila, Catherine of Siena, and Térèse of Lisieux. There's some irony in this title for these women, as the church has used words of Paul as an argument against ordination of women: Paul's words are usually interpreted to forbid women from teaching in the church.

MIRABAI (CA. 1498–CA. 1546)

Mirabai was a Brahmin princess in the northern part of India, whose love for the divine drove her to seek enlightenment. Traditions say that in approximately 1498 in northern India, Mira was born in Chaukari village in the small independent state of Merta in

Rajasthan state. She was born to the Rathpore clan descended from the founder of Jodhpur. Her family ruled Merta and were great devotees of the Hindu god Vishnu. Her name is also spelled Meera.

Though she became an immensely popular religious poet and one of the most significant saints in the Bhakti tradition, there are few facts definitively known about her. During Mira's lifetime, there was great political and social unrest because of Muslim invasions. The Hindu population of northern India was struggling to maintain its culture and livelihoods.

A wandering sadhu (a religious ascetic) came to their family home when young Mira was three years old, and gave to her father, Ratan Singh, a little idol of the Hindu deity Krishna. Her father accepted it as a special blessing, but at first he didn't want to give it to his daughter, thinking she would not appreciate it. But at first sight, young Mira was charmed by the doll, refusing to eat until it was given to her.

To the child, this doll embodied the deity. She resolved to make Krishna her lifelong friend and love. There is a legend that while she was still very young, Mira saw a wedding procession going past in the street. She asked her mother in innocence, "Who will be my husband?" Her mother's half-serious, half-joking reply was, "You already have your husband, Sri Krishna." In this tale, Mira's mother was supportive of her daughter and of her displays of religious tendencies even at a young age.

Mirabai expressed her religious devotion to the Hindu god Krishna through the writing of more than one thousand bhajans, or sacred songs. Many of her poems are still performed today.

Unfortunately, her mother passed away while Mira was only a child. Her father was occupied with the responsibilities of war, and he let the child be raised by her grandparents. Mira's education was a customary one for royal families in that part of the world: as well as reading and writing, she was taught the scriptures, music, archery, fencing, and how to ride horses and drive chariots. She was even trained in the use of weapons, because this was a time of war. Mild mannered and soft-spoken, Mira had a sweet nature and a melodious voice. She was called Mirabai (also spelled Meera Bai), for Bai was often added to the name of a lady as a sign of respect. The fame of her beauty spread to nearby kingdoms.

As time went on, Mirabai's religious devotion was influenced by a number of her male relatives, who were devotees of a Hindu form of mysticism called Bhakti, in which a person reveres the divine through love, without any barriers of caste, color, or gender. Her faith became an all-consuming relationship, which made her reluctant to marry. When she was a child, her family had arranged that she would marry Prince Bhoj Raj, eldest son of the king of Chittor. Luckily, the prince and his father understood her devotion and respected it, so she obeyed her father and grandfather, marrying at about the age of fourteen. Marriage into this influential Hindu family elevated her social status, but the luxuries of the palace were not important to Mirabai.

Unfortunately, after five years her husband died of wounds he received in battle. As his widow, Mira chose to live as the devoted spouse of her divine lord. Mira attended religious meetings called *Satsangs*, where she would worship with others, singing and dancing. Stories say that sometimes she wore ankle bells and held castanets or little cymbals. She also gave her time and energies to caring for the religious poor, in what was seen as a denial of her caste and royal privilege. Mira's father-in-law became her protector but died also shortly after. Her husband's brother then became king of Chittor. He and the rest of her late husband's family wanted Mira to renounce all public displays of her faith. A highborn princess was expected to live in seclusion and keep aloof from the common people in lower castes. As a wife, she was expected to pay homage to the god and goddess her husband's family revered. As a widow, she was expected to commit *sati*—suicide—by throwing herself on the funeral pyre for her late husband. When she refused, several attempts were made on her life. The details of these failed attempts are legendary and reminiscent of similar miracles in the lives of Catholic saints.

On the advice of a spiritual counsellor, Mira left the palace and returned to her family home. She found that her birthplace was not a place of safety for her, either, now that her uncle was the ruler. She traveled then, throughout northern India. "She was born a princess but forsook the pleasures of a palace for begging on the streets of Brindaban," wrote one biographer. There are stories of ladies who were glad to have her visit as she traveled. "She lived during a time of war and spiritual decline, but her life offered a shining example of the purest devotion."[7]

Her love for Krishna was the central theme for some thirteen hundred sacred songs she composed, called *bhajans*. Some scholars consider that many songs by her admirers have become associated with the two to three hundred songs Mirabai actually wrote. These songs used everyday language in a simple rhythm, with a repeated refrain. She wrote of longing for union with the divine, at times expressing the pain of separation or the ecstasy of holy union. Her sweet-natured poetry was charming for many people, and became part of a mystic tradition. Her popularity has lasted five hundred years, and many of her devotional poems are still sung today.

Traditions say that Mirabai spent the last years of her life as a pilgrim in Dwarka Gujarat, and that in 1546 while she was singing in a temple, Sri Krishna appeared before her in his subtle form. He opened up his heart, and as Mirabai died, she melted into his heart. It is said she left her body while in the highest state of consciousness.

Mohandas Gandhi considered Mirabai an example "of a woman who has the right to choose her own path, forsake a life of luxury, and in nonviolent resistance find liberation."[8] The role that Mirabai continues to play in her culture and literature is important, but there is a social dichotomy in the way her memory is invoked. A reference to Mirabai is still used to influence women. Sometimes a woman is said to be like Mirabai, meaning that she is unwomanly and must conform to tradition. It's a warning to straighten up or be destined for trouble! There's also a contrasting way in which her name is used. When others say that a woman is like Mirabai, they mean that she has strength of character and is a free spirit who knows what she believes and stands up for it.

CHAPTER THREE

WOMEN WRITING DURING THE ENLIGHTENMENT

The Italian Renaissance brought a transition from medieval times to the Early Modern Period in Europe. This time of renewed technological development, cultural innovations, and government reorganization came later for northern European countries, where the English Civil Wars, the American Revolution, and the French Revolution all marked great changes, particularly for people who were educated and prosperous. This chapter discusses a sample of women writers from the Age of Reason.

MARY WOLLSTONECRAFT (1759–1797)

A pioneering English feminist wrote the earliest works of modern feminist philosophy, which shaped

own interest. Women weren't automatically paragons of virtue, either, as she noted in her fiction. Somehow, the cultural narrative of her society failed to connect for Austen, and she could not propagate it.

There was no revolution for Austen to join to improve the world, no Occupy or Solidarity movement. There were no books to teach her what was wrong with society and how to improve human relations. Instead, she pursued the only revolution available to her: she wrote comic novels about manners, which exposed society as hypocritical. She was in her way, a fifth columnist. Her six books simultaneously depicted behaviors of her time accurately while turning the cultural narrative on its head through her female protagonists being active agents in their own lives. Austen had few fellow travelers when she began, but as her fame grew there were at least readers who wanted her kind of novels. Rudyard Kipling was later to write about the Janeites, praising the dedicated fans of books about human interaction rather than adventure.

Austen's novels continue to touch audiences, both in print and on the big and small screens. *Pride and Prejudice* was so revolutionary in approach that two hundred years later it was lampooned in a book and film called *Pride and Prejudice and Zombies*—without losing its essential qualities or compromising its characters. Her novel *Emma* inspired the cult comedy movie *Clueless*.

ELIZABETH BARRETT BROWNING (1806–1861)

Shakespeare was honored during his life for his plays and poetry. It took two centuries after Shakespeare's death for a female poet to rise to a similar kind of public praise. That poet was Elizabeth Barrett Browning.

Elizabeth Barrett was born in 1806 to an English aristocratic family. The Barrett family had become wealthy from owning sugar plantations in Jamaica. Elizabeth's father chose to live in England and raise his children there, managing his plantations at a distance. Elizabeth was the first child in the Barrett family line to be born in England in more than two hundred years. She and her siblings were forbidden to marry by their father. This kind of family tyranny was legal and had been for centuries. Mr. Barrett's tyranny came from the fear that a dark-skinned grandchild would reveal his secret: his Creole origins.

Educated at home, young Elizabeth was a bright student

The love story of Elizabeth Barrett and Robert Browning yielded some of the world's most beautiful love poems.

of the classics, including the sonnets of Petrarch. Unfortunately, she developed a lung ailment at fourteen. At fifteen, she suffered a spinal injury while saddling a pony. Elizabeth Barrett had to endure her ill health as well as her father's dominance over the household. She was bitterly opposed to slavery and horrified that her father's plantations profited at the expense of slaves. For years she rarely left her room, not even to go to church.

In her room, she wrote poetry that became increasingly popular in magazines. The books of verse she wrote were praised by critics and became widely read. Elizabeth Barrett became a celebrity, more than a bit mysterious as she rarely left her room or her father's house.

When she was introduced to emerging poet Robert Browning in 1845, they began an extraordinary courtship kept secret from her father. Barrett was already considered England's greatest living poet, while Browning (six years younger) had not yet achieved success as a poet. His second book had earned him the "reputation of being the most pretentious and abstruse poet in England."[5] Their immediate intellectual and romantic attraction blossomed. During the next twenty months, they exchanged nearly six hundred letters.

When they eloped in 1846, Barrett left her sickroom behind. It didn't matter that her father disinherited her. She had income from her writing, and now the love of her husband. In Italy, when Browning began to find his own writing success and the couple's son was born, Barrett gave him a sonnet series that she had written during their courtship. It was published under the title *Sonnets from the Portuguese*.

Poetry written by women during the Victorian era typically had humble and modest female speakers. In this sonnet series, Barrett created an appropriately modest narrator, but one who challenges convention by addressing her beloved as though she felt empowered rather than only humble. She was an innovator in the construction of a sonnet, challenging convention with her female narrative persona as well as in the use of enjambment and *voltas*.

Their son published his parents' correspondence after their deaths. Among many readers and critics, the story of their courting has taken attention away from Barrett's sonnets and other writing. As one scholar observed, "The letters are the communication between two people and the sonnets are the communication of one woman trying to articulate love."[6]

It was in courting Elizabeth Barrett that Robert Browning found his artistic center. With their union, he gained confidence that gradually transformed his new writing—and in particular, critical opinions of his work—into much more popular and praised verses. In time, his reputation grew to match hers and continued to do so after their deaths, until the emergence of feminist literary theory brought renewed interpretations of Barrett's poetry as superior work.

HARRIET BEECHER STOWE (1811–1896)

A working writer for women's magazines wrote a serial novel that became a focus for the social movement against slavery. Harriet Beecher Stowe was born in Connecticut as Harriet Elizabeth Beecher, one of many children of Lyman Beecher, an academic administrator, and Roxana Foote. Though young Harriet was only five when her mother died, she had loving care from her father and her older sister Catherine, and her father's second wife.

Her childhood was spent in Litchfield, where ministers, judges, and lawyers would visit the Beecher home. Law students boarded with the family, and her father encouraged them and his children to debate at the dinner table.[7] When

The abolitionist Harriet Beecher Stowe educated Americans about the horrors of slavery with her novel *Uncle Tom's Cabin*.

about twelve, she went to Hartford, where her sister Catherine had opened a school. Young Harriet was a fine scholar, though absentminded and moody.

In 1832, twenty-one-year-old Harriet Beecher moved with her family to Cincinnati, Ohio, where she joined a literary society and began writing for magazines and newspapers. Her style of "Western humor and colloquial language—assumed to have been the innovations of Samuel Clemens—began to appear in 1833, two years before his birth,"[8] noted one biographer. She married Calvin Stowe, a theology professor. It was in Cincinnati that she met fugitive slaves for the first time. Many of her works were written to combat slavery, which she considered the greatest injustice of the time.

The mother of seven children, Stowe suffered tremendous loss when her eighteen-month-old son died of cholera in 1949. That loss became one of the inspirations for *Uncle Tom's Cabin* because she felt it helped her understand the pain that enslaved mothers felt when their children were taken from them to be sold.

The first installment of *Uncle Tom's Cabin* appeared on June 5, 1851, in the antislavery newspaper, *The National Era*. Stowe avidly read freedom narratives and antislavery newspapers for firsthand accounts as she composed her story. Friends and family sent her what information they could find. Stowe expected *Uncle Tom's Cabin or Life Among the Lowly* to be in three or four installments, but in all she wrote over forty. In 1852, the serial was collected into a two-volume book, which became a best seller in America, Britain, Europe, and Asia, was and translated into over sixty languages.

The novel brought not only financial security but also enabled Stowe to write full-time. She began publishing multiple works per year, starting with *A Key to Uncle Tom's Cabin*, which documented the case histories on which she had based her novel. Stowe wrote later of this book and her other writings on slavery: "I wrote what I did because as a woman, as a mother, I was oppressed and broken-hearted with the sorrows and injustice I saw, because as a Christian I felt the dishonor to Christianity—because as a lover of my county, I trembled at the coming day of wrath."[9]

For the rest of her life, Stowe continued to write and work to improve society. After her husband retired from teaching theology, Stowe went on two speaking tours for her books. She improved the art museum at Wadsworth Atheneum and cofounded the Hartford Art School. After the American Civil War, her brother opened a school in Florida to teach emancipated people, so Stowe and her husband traveled to Florida each winter for fifteen years to help him teach. In all, Harriet Beecher Stowe's writing career spanned fifty-one years, during which time she published thirty books and countless short stories, poems, articles, and hymns.

CHAPTER FOUR

WOMEN WRITERS IN THE INDUSTRIAL REVOLUTION

During the 1800s in English-speaking countries, there were gradual changes in social attitudes toward women writers. Over time, it became easier and more socially acceptable for women to be published authors, particularly if they wrote about women's concerns. Some female writers used pseudonyms for anonymity, to fit within cultural paradigms for authors, or to hide their femininity. As it became more ordinary for women writers to be published, some of the ideas they discussed began to enter the mainstream of literature and culture, or at least to challenge it.

CHARLOTTE BRONTË (1816–1855)

Four lonely children who made up fantasy stories became a family of writers with fame outlasting their short lives. The story of Charlotte Brontë as a person and as a writer is the story of her siblings as well. Born in 1816, Charlotte Brontë was the third daughter at birth, but she became the eldest surviving daughter of her Anglo-Irish family.

The family name was originally Brunty, something far more Irish than her father, the Reverend Patrick Brontë, allowed. He changed it to Brontë as part of his social-climbing ambition and became the vicar in a village parish in Yorkshire. After the death of his wife, Marie, from a lung ailment (perhaps cancer or tuberculosis), he sent his four older daughters to a school for the daughters of clergy. Crowded living conditions there in a damp, unheated building were terrible, and the two eldest Brontë girls died of tuberculosis. The younger two, Charlotte and Emily, were sent home, but they were already ill. Their brother, Branwell, and sister Anne caught tuberculosis as well.

The Brontë siblings had a lonely childhood, with an aged aunt looking after their isolated home, and a father who persisted in middle-class dreams on a parson's modest income. All four children wrote stories in notebooks, and they invented role-playing games, acted out on maps in an under-furnished room. As young adults, Charlotte and her siblings realized that their stories were more satisfying than the popular novels they had read.

The Brontë sisters began sending their manuscripts to publishers and became published authors. The modest amount they earned from royalties was a welcome addition to their family income. Charlotte was the most prolific and successful of the three sisters. All three used pen names for anonymity, to protect their father's reputation from the scandal of commercial fiction. Charlotte was Currer Bell, Emily was Ellis Bell, and Anne was Acton Bell—three male names because women were not expected to take an interest in writing fiction, nor to have any talent for it. Branwell was not published, but his juvenile writing is still studied.

On the advice of a friend, Charlotte and Emily went to Brussels, spending half a year at a school owned by Zoë Héger, where the sisters could acquire a bit more polish to their French. While there, Charlotte was deeply impressed by the husband of the school's headmistress. Constantin Héger was charismatic and widely read, and he recognized Charlotte's intelligence. Impressed that he loved books as she did, and

The lonely childhoods Charlotte Brontë and her sisters experienced bred rich writers' imaginations.

starved for affection and romance, Charlotte felt a passionate longing for him.[1]

With hindsight, Brontë realized her return the next year to teach at the *Pensionnat Héger* was a mistake. She had fallen in love with someone who would never see her in a romantic light. Héger had impressive intellect and spirit, and was the first person outside her family to take her seriously, as a potential equal. But as his junior colleague, Brontë was treated more formally, as the Hégers kept her at a distance.

In frustration, Brontë turned to writing again, and succeeded in finding a publisher. Her novels were energized with active heroines and strong romantic interests, to an extent that was scandalous for the time. In all the books she came to write, Héger was the inspiration for her choleric, dark, and fascinating men. The modern genres of gothic fiction and romance novels, and also the soft-core pornography of the twentieth century, owe much to the influence of Brontë's writing.

Brontë had chosen a pen name not only to hide her identity, but to escape notice as a woman writer. "I wished critics would judge me as a writer, not as a woman."[2] When she was revealed to be Currer Bell, to her disappointment the critical discussion of her works focused on her femininity more than the artistic merit of her writing or her confident female protagonists.

In one dreadful nine-month period, Brontë lost her brother and her sisters to tuberculosis and its complications. For five years, Brontë kept house for her blind father, while working on her writing and making a few trips to London to see her publisher. She married her father's curate (church assistant) in part to make life easier for her father. "After the deaths of Branwell, Emily, and Anne, I think Charlotte was just sort of subsisting, emotionally. Arthur Nicholls was a very odd choice for her to marry, in terms of his lack of imagination," Claire Harman said in a radio interview about her biography released on the two-hundredth anniversary of Charlotte Brontë's birth. "To her credit, she did find some contentment in the marriage and was comforted by his company—though only for a short time."[3]

Though it was not a love match, she had respect for how her husband's love for her made him vulnerable to her. Brontë was the heroine of her own story, and while she didn't have grand adventures, she did not let her intellect keep her from becoming as satisfied with life as a heroine in one of her own novels. She came to feel comforted by their marriage. During her first pregnancy, Brontë was terribly ill with prolonged morning sickness. Unrelenting nausea would not allow her to eat or drink well, which caused her death before her thirty-ninth birthday.

The sisters became subject to the kind of cult fascination that surrounds Elvis or other performers who die before their time. Since the first biography of the Brontës, many others have appeared; each reflects changing attitudes of the reading public about the role of women as writers, about sexuality, and about personality.

MARY ANN EVANS/GEORGE ELIOT (1819–1880)

A provincial girl transformed herself into one of the better-known intellectuals of the nineteenth century. She became an "English Victorian novelist who developed the method of psychological analysis characteristic of modern fiction."[4]

Born in Warwickshire at an estate of her father's employer, Mary Ann Evans went at nine years old to be a boarder at Mrs. Wallington's School at Nuneaton for four years. There the principal governess, Maria Lewis, taught young Mary Ann a strong evangelical piety. The last school she attended was at Coventry, led by daughters of a Baptist minister, where she learned to read French and Italian. She took to wearing severe plain dresses and kept very busy doing good works. At her mother's death, her father brought her home to keep house, but he allowed her to take lessons in Latin and German.

Several books she read on the relation between science and the Bible gave her the troubling thoughts the books were trying to discourage. In 1841, Evans met Charles Bray, a self-taught free-thinker, radical activist, and a prosperous ribbon manufacturer. When Evans read a book *An Inquiry Concerning the Origin of Christianity*, by Bray's brother-in-law Charles Hennell, it motivated her to break with orthodoxy. Bray and his wife, along with Hennell and his wife, introduced Evans to ideas in strong disagreement with her Tory father's provincial views on politics and religion.

Evans took on from Hennell's wife, Rufa, the translating of D. F. Strauss's book *The Life of Jesus Critically Examined*, which became a profoundly influential book for English rationalism. Rufa Hennell's father, R. H. Brabant, invited Evans to visit at his home in Devizes, where together they read German and Greek and discussed theology on long walks. When Brabant's wife became jealous of this closeness, Evans was made to end her visit early. Later Evans drew on this humiliating experience when writing her novel *Middlemarch*.

When she told her father in 1842 that she intended not to attend church again, he was furious. Their argument continued for several months before they compromised. He allowed her to think what she pleased so long as she appeared respectably at church, and that

Intellectual giant Mary Ann Evans chose a man's name, George Eliot, under which to write her masterpiece, *Middlemarch*.

arrangement continued until his death in 1849.

Her inheritance was an income of £100 a year, only enough to live on if she paid room and board in the homes of generous friends. She found writing, translating, and editing work to make her living. "Having refused a marriage proposal . . . in her mid-twenties, Eliot had entanglements in her early thirties with men to whom she wasn't married . . . and with men who were married to someone else, including John Chapman, the publisher of the *Westminster Review*, and Eliot's employer and landlord," wrote one biographer. "Both Chapman's wife and his live-in mistress, the Chapman children's governess, were so vexed by the attentions that he was paying to his interesting lodger that Eliot was obliged to move out, at least until Chapman's need for her editing skills overruled the preferences of his womenfolk."[5]

Evans chose a male pen name, George Eliot, because she was not writing as a woman about the concerns of women, which were marginalized from mainstream literature. In time, she became both successful and well known. Her book *Middlemarch* is widely considered the best novel in the English language, not because of its intricate plot but because of its faultless depiction of people in every class of life.

The great love of her life was unable to get a legal divorce, so she lived with him for twenty-five years. "Light and easily broken ties are what I neither desire theoretically nor could live for practically," she told one censorious friend after she eloped with George Lewes. "Women who are satisfied with such ties do *not* act as I have done — they obtain what they desire and are still invited to dinner."[6]

Rather than the ideal feminine beauty, Evans was considered exceedingly plain. People were not kind about her appearance. After their first meeting, "magnificently ugly, deliciously hideous" is what author Henry James wrote of her. He added, "Behold me, literally in love with this great horse-faced bluestocking!" He noted as well something interesting about her so-called ugliness: when conversing, her expression showed so much sympathy and tenderness that she made a lasting impression of beauty. "Eliot was possessed of a radiant, luminous intelligence that outshone her perceived deficits," concludes a present-day journalist, "that rendered irrelevant the small-minded criticisms of her character and visage to which she was subject for much of her life."[7]

Middlemarch, published in eight parts during 1871–72, "is by general consent George Eliot's masterpiece. Under her hand the novel had developed from a mere entertainment into a highly intellectual form of art," wrote one scholar. "The story depends not on close-knit intrigue but on showing the incalculably diffusive effect of the unhistoric acts of those who 'lived faithfully a hidden life and rest in unvisited tombs.'"[8]

EMILY DICKINSON (1830–1886)

Emily Dickinson led one of the most homebound lives of any great poet, spending most of her life not only in her hometown, but within her family home. Born in Amherst, Massachusetts, to a prominent but not wealthy family descended from Puritans, Emily Dickinson had an older brother and younger sister. Their father was treasurer of Amherst College, founded by his own father. He took a great interest in the children's education, even when he traveled as a state legislator and a congressman. In her later correspondence, Emily always wrote of him in a warm manner but represented her mother as cold and aloof.

At age ten, young Emily began seven years of studies at the Amherst Academy, learning English and classical literature, Latin, botany, geology, history, philosophy, and arithmetic. She was an excellent student despite missing some terms due to illness. The death from typhus of Sophia Holland, her second cousin and friend, affected fourteen-year-old Emily so much that her parents sent her to stay with family in Boston to recover. She attended Mount Holyoke Female Seminary for only ten months before her brother came to take her home, perhaps because of her health or rebellion against the evangelical fervor at the school.

Her journals and poetry reveal Dickinson's profound love for God, even though she was at odds with the church and the unforgiving religion she was taught as a child. There was a Christian revival in her hometown during her teenage years; she felt the attraction but came to resist and distrust orthodox attitudes. As an adult, she read a great deal and took to spending hours outdoors on her father's land, walking over hills near her home and finding reverence in nature. Several of her poems express religious feelings, which were positive, sustaining, and surprising to her after learning as a child to fear hellfire and damnation.[9]

As was expected of an unmarried grown woman, Dickinson lived modestly in her father's home with a minimal income, as did her sister. The reason Dickinson chose not to marry is not recorded in her notebooks or journals. Some of her biographers have suggested that she found herself unexpectedly in love with a

Prolific poet Emily Dickinson was not well known during her lifetime, but her poetry has never gone out of print.

Massachusetts Supreme Court judge in a nearby town, but the match was not suitable because of the difference in age and social station between them.

For much of her adult life, Dickinson was agoraphobic, to use the modern term.[10] There were entire years when Dickinson wouldn't even leave the house, and for many more years she would walk no farther than the fence around her father's grounds. Yet once a year she would invite in all the neighbors in the village and surrounding area and be the perfect host. When her mother became chronically ill and could not be left alone, Dickinson was there for her and to keep house. She and her sister kept the garden in fine condition. As well as knowing everyone in her village, Dickinson had a few friends who were poets, with whom she corresponded regularly.

Because Dickinson released few of her poems for publication, she was almost unknown as a writer during her lifetime. In her poetry Dickinson developed an aphoristic style, using slant rhymes and forceful iambic meter interrupted by dashes. Her poems typically lack titles, contain short lines, and have unconventional capitalization and punctuation. English Literature students joke that one can sing any of Emily Dickinson's poems to the tune of "The Yellow Rose of Texas"—and they're not wrong, at least for many of the poems, though the tune sounds bizarre with her recurring themes of death and immortality.

In the opinion of a scholar writing a hundred years later, when Dickinson wrote about loving God, she was showing her Neoplatonic beliefs about perceiving the true nature of the universe by seeing it in distorted reflections in the natural world. "The finite self's desire for the divine Other is in the nature of things," Roland Hagenbuchle wrote. "Whereas Kierkegaard found the Other in the savior figure of the Biblical God, Dickinson, at odds with religious orthodoxy, was thrown back on the evidence of the soul's desire for the missing Other."[11]

The Romantic poets had faith in the creative potential of the self but were particularly aware of its precarious status. They were disturbed by the idea that for each of us, the self is separate from its transcendental origin with the Divine; the Romantics felt alienated, as though free will was not effective. "With Emily Dickinson, this sense of alienation is raised to a new pitch," according to Hagenbuchle. "Dickinson's cultural heritage—especially the paradoxical nature of Puritan selfhood along with the Transcendentalist emphasis on 'Self-Reliance'—radicalized the problem for her, and she was forced to look for new tactics in her effort to reconstruct a viable New-England self."[12]

Dickinson was influenced by Shakespeare, the book of Revelations in the Bible, the Reverend Charles Wadsworth, whom she met on a trip to Philadelphia with her mother and sister, Henry Wadsworth Longfellow, Charlotte Brontë, and the Metaphysical poets of seventeenth-century England: John Keats, and Robert and Elizabeth Barrett Browning. Though she was familiar with works of the transcendentalist writers only a few miles away in Concord, Massachusetts, Dickinson did not consider herself one of them.

At fifty-five years old, Dickinson died in her family home of Bright's disease, or chronic kidney disease. During her lifetime, Dickinson allowed only a dozen or so of her poems to be published in various magazines and anthologies. Among Dickinson's papers after her death, her younger sister, Lavinia, found nearly eighteen hundred poems in notebooks and forty neatly handwritten volumes. Two of Dickinson's poet friends were familiar with her published poetry. When organizing her poetry notebooks for posthumous publication, her friends edited several of the earlier poems for the first two volumes, replacing her unconventional use of capital letters and dashes with more conventional punctuation. Later volumes were more true to Dickinson's handwritten notebooks. "There is no better example of the New England tendency to moral revelry than this last pale Indian-summer flower of Puritanism," wrote literary historian Norman Foerster. "[H]er place in American letters will be inconspicuous but secure."[13] Her poetry has never gone out of print.

LOUISA MAY ALCOTT (1832–1888)

A working author of potboiler melodramas, Louisa May Alcott achieved her goal to earn a living writing works of literary merit under her own name. Born in Germantown, Pennsylvania, Louisa May Alcott was the daughter of Abigail May and Amos Bronson Alcott. The Alcott children were raised on their mother's practical Christianity and taught at home by their Transcendentalist philosopher father. Young Louisa was a tomboy who ran races, climbed trees, and jumped fences with her three sisters and the boys and girls of their neighborhoods in Boston and Concord, Massachusetts. She studied also with family friends, including Henry David Thoreau, who took her on nature rambles, and Ralph Waldo Emerson, who let her use his library.

independence. She met the demand for more books with a steady stream of novels and short stories meant for young readers and based on her family life. The novels she wrote for adults were not as popular. In all, she wrote over thirty books and collections of stories. Many of her books are still popular today. Alcott died two days after her father, in 1888. Her grave is in Sleepy Hollow Cemetery in Concord. Her home, Orchard House, has over fifty thousand visitors a year and is maintained by a memorial association, which holds a teacher's institute and conversational series each year.

TEKAHIONWAKE/E. PAULINE JOHNSON (1861–1913)

Popular in the late nineteenth century, Tekahionwake was a Canadian writer and performer of mixed race. In Mohawk her name was Tekahionwake (which means "double life"), and in English it was Emily Pauline Johnson (which means "striving little child of God's gift"). She was born March 10, 1861, on the Six Nations Indian Reserve near the small city of Brampton in the British crown colony of Upper Canada, which six years later became the province of Ontario when Canada was declared a nation. Her mother was Emily Susanna Howells Johnson, a Quaker immigrant from England who had come to the American colonies in 1832 as a child with her own family, before coming to Canada. Her father was George Henry Martin Johnson, a hereditary Mohawk chief of the Six Nations Confederacy; the mother of George Johnson was a Dutch girl who had been taken captive and assimilated as Mohawk after adoption by a Wolf clan family.[16]

The marriage of Emily and George Johnson had been opposed by both of their families. Mixed marriages were not uncommon but not accepted in society at the time; but the couple became acknowledged as a leading family in the new nation of Canada. The Johnsons were well known and enjoyed a high standard of living in their home, called Chiefswood, constructed in 1856 on a 225-acre estate on the reserve. They entertained many influential guests such as Alexander Graham Bell, noted painters and anthropologists, and Lord Dufferin, Governor General of Canada, and his lady.

The youngest of four children, young Pauline was a sickly child who did not attend the residential school for First Nations children in Brantford. Education for the Johnson children was mostly at home and informal. As a child, Pauline was taught by her mother or by a series of governesses, and during a few years at the small day school on the reserve. Self-directed reading in the extensive library of the family

MISS E. PAULINE JOHNSON.

HAMILTON, ONT.   BRANTFORD, ONT.

Pauline Johnson, also known as Tekahionwake, achieved success as a poet and performer.

home made her familiar with the works of Browning, Keats, Tennyson, Milton, and Byron. In particular, she enjoyed reading tales that colonialist writers such as Longfellow and John Richardson had created about Native people.[17]

As an adult, Johnson carefully wrote poetry of two distinct kinds. One was an homage to her First Nations heritage, and the other was conventional literary verse expected then of an English lady. She self-published volumes of her poetry and set up public readings for a fee. For the first poems, she wore a buckskin dress she made and decorated herself, in a style a little like First Nations regalia; after a short break she would go on to read her literary verses dressed in a floor-length ball gown.

As a performer, Johnson was a success. It was rare and remarkable at the time for a woman to perform so independently in public without being simply an actress and a fallen woman. Johnson earned enough to buy and maintain a home, where she lived with her widowed mother and sister. "She traveled extensively across Canada, the U.S. and England performing her poetry—both First Nations inspired poems while wearing traditional dress as well as more conventional writing while donning ballgowns—at the turn of the nineteenth century,"[18] noted the Canadian Broadcasting Corporation when reporting on the 2014 premiere of the opera *Pauline*, based on her multicultural identity and her art, written by Margaret Atwood and composer Tobin Stokes.

"One of the fine lines that she walked was her reputation," according to Atwood. "In Victorian times, reputation—for a woman—meant sexual reputation. And that had to be spotless. So that explains why her sister, when Pauline was dead, burned all the papers. Because she also did have a double life."[19]

During the last years of her life, Johnson lived in the city of Vancouver. Before her death in 1913 at the age of fifty-one, she suffered terribly from breast cancer; the available treatment of crude surgery and morphine was not sufficient to control her pain. She was buried in Stanley Park, where in 1922 a monument was raised to her memory, near Lost Lagoon, which she described in her poetry.

On the centennial of her birth in 1961, a commemorative postage stamp was issued with her name and image, which made her the first author, the first aboriginal Canadian, and the first woman other than the queen to be honored this way by Canada. Critics began to recognize her literary works at that time, whereas previously she had been neglected as primarily a performer only. She was regarded as neither sufficiently interesting as an English Canadian poet nor sufficiently Native to excite the interest of critics. Schools have been named in her honor, as well as anthologies of new writing by multicultural authors.

CHAPTER FIVE

WOMEN WRITING IN THE TWENTIETH CENTURY

By the twentieth century, books, magazines, and newspapers were widely available, thanks to affordable printing and distribution. Public libraries and public schools made a high-school education a possibility for more people than ever before. The greatest inequalities between rich and poor, among races, or between men and women became more equal.

During this century, published authors who were women were no longer rare oddities. Some wrote from their own experience about ordinary lives of people, whether prosperous or working-class; some had the benefit of university educations and wrote as scholars among peers. It was still not ordinary for a writer to be a woman, but women were participating in writing and publishing in all kinds of ways. The women profiled in this chapter changed social conventions and the world at large.

VIRGINIA WOOLF (1882–1941)

One of the greatest narrative writers in the English language struggled all her life to survive loss and horror. Born at home in the Kensington neighborhood of London, Adeline Virginia Stephen was the third of four children born to her parents. Her father, Leslie Stephen, was a man of letters from a family distinguished for public service in Victorian England, with a daughter from his first marriage. Her mother, Julia, was from a family noted for their beauty, with three children of her own from her first marriage.

Julia and Leslie Stephen lived with all eight of their children and a number of servants. Many writers visited their home. The family spent long summer holidays in Cornwall, which made lasting impressions on young Virginia. Later in life, Woolf saw herself as descended from both a male and female inheritance of distinct talents in the arts.

Determined to be a writer, young Virginia made good use of her father's extensive library, to which she had uncensored access. She never went to school, and had a patchwork education by tutors.[1] Her older sister Vanessa trained as a painter, and their two brothers went away to school and then to Cambridge. Their brother Thorby's friends became the core of Virginia's literary circle, which would be known as the Bloomsbury Group.

The unexpected death of her mother in 1895 caused Virginia to have a mental breakdown. Years later she gave a disturbing talk to a Freudian group called the Memoir Club, describing how her older half-brother had molested her, coming to her bedroom at night from childhood to late adolescence. Virginia had a second breakdown on the death of her father in 1904, and with her recovery began writing book reviews for two journals. When her sister arranged for the four siblings to move into a home in the Bloomsbury neighborhood, Thorby invited his friends to visit on Thursday evenings. This informal salon continued after his death in 1907.

Leonard Woolf, one of her late brother's friends, proposed marriage to Virginia, and in 1912 they were married in a registry office. Both husband and wife planned to earn their living by writing. Unfortunately, another mental breakdown delayed the publication of Woolf's first novel until 1915. "Nowhere do we have a more detailed and powerfully moving record of repeated episodes of decline

Novelist Virginia Woolf is one of the few women writers of her time to be part of the modern literary canon.

into and recovery from mental illness than that in the life of Virginia Woolf," wrote Maxwell Bennett, calling her "perhaps the finest narrative writer in English in the twentieth century."[2]

A small hand printing press was a useful hobby for the couple, and good therapy for Woolf as she recovered. Hogarth Press was named for their house in Surrey where they lived at the time. Her second novel was released in 1919, but after that Woolf hand printed and published her own writing. She wrote several short stories and novels in an experimental, modernist style throughout the 1920s. As Hogarth Press grew, by 1932 the Woolfs became publishers more than writers.

The Second World War was another dreadful stress for Woolf, who endured depressive phases as the Battle for Britain went on, frighteningly close. In 1940 the Blitz bombed the Woolfs out of their London home, twice. They retreated to a small village house they had bought in Sussex for summer use. Woolf took twenty-four volumes of her diary, intending to edit and complete her memoirs. Even in Sussex, German planes droned overhead. It wasn't surprising when Woolf became mentally ill again. She left a suicide note for her husband and drowned herself in the River Ouse on March 28, 1941.

In her work, Woolf emphasized a stream of consciousness in her narratives. "In her essays and diaries and fiction, in her reading of history, in her feminism, in her politics, 'life-writing' as she herself called it, was a perpetual preoccupation," wrote a biographer. "Virginia Woolf was an autobiographer who never published an autobiography; she was an egotist who loathed egotism. . . . She is always trying to work out what happens to . . . the 'damned egotistical self.'"[3] She strove to get at the essence of personality. Two lectures that Woolf gave in 1928 at women's colleges in Cambridge were the basis for her book *A Room of One's Own*, which discussed the historical economic and social underpinning for women's writing.

ANNA AKHMATOVA (1889–1966)

As Anna Akhmatova learned, suppression and censorship affect nations and cultures, not just poets. Anna Andreevna Gorenko was born at Bolshoy Fontan, near Odessa, Russian Empire (now Ukraine), on the Black Sea. When she was nearly a year old, her family moved near Saint Petersburg. Both her mother, Inna Eramovna Stogova, and her father, Andrey Antonovich Gorenko, a naval engineer, were descended from Russian nobles. Her childhood does not appear to have been happy, as her parents separated in 1905.

Inspired by reading Pushkin and Racine, young Anna began writing poetry at age eleven. She was published in her teens, but none of her juvenilia has been found. She was educated at Tsarskoye Selo, near Saint Petersburg, and at Kiev. When she told her parents that she wanted to be a poet, her father disapproved, saying that he didn't want to see any poetry published under his respectable name. Anna chose her Tartar grandmother's maiden name as a pen name.

In 1910 Akhmatova married Nikolai Gumilyov, cofounder of the Guild of Poets, a literary movement advocating craftmanship, later called Acmeism. She impressed the literary circles in Saint Petersburg with her artistic integrity and aristocratic manners and was magnetically alluring to intellectual men. Her first collection of poems was published the year her son Lev was born, in 1912. By the time her second collection was published in 1914, thousands of Russian women were writing poems in her honor.[4]

But her husband did not take her poems seriously; he left her after their honeymoon to tour in Africa. They were divorced in 1918. Gumilov was later arrested and executed in 1921 on trumped-up charges of being part of a Monarchist conspiracy. Akhmatova married Vladimir Shileiko, but they separated in 1920 and in 1928 were divorced.

After 1922, Akhmatova was condemned as a bourgeois element, and publication of her poetry was banned. All of her literary friends were similarly repressed, imprisoned, or forced to emigrate. She earned her living by writing essays for scholarly journals, memoirs, and translations.

Akhmatova's third husband, Nikolai Punin, and her son, Lev, were arrested in 1935, as were several friends. Lev was released when his mother wrote to Stalin, but he was arrested again in 1938. He served in the air force on his release.

Akhmatova was allowed to publish a new collection of poems in 1940, and during the Second World War her patriotic poems appeared on the front page of *Pravda*. But in 1946, visits from the political philosopher Sir Isaiah Berlin put her in disgrace. Her poems were banned from publication. Her son was arrested again in 1949 and spent fifteen years in a Siberian gulag. Akhmatova was able to secure his release only by writing several poems praising Stalin. Her husband died in a Siberian camp in the 1950s.

Anna Akhmatova's distinctive poems reflected the terrors of Russia's Stalinist regime.

Akhmatova continued to compose. When she went out, the KGB searched her modest home and confiscated anything written. Rarely would a friend visit, and while making tea she would write out a poem from memory. The friend would commit the poem to memory and burn it, while maintaining a conversation for the benefit of the KGB's listening devices. Her poems circulated in *samizdat* (a secret system) and by word of mouth as a symbol of suppressed Russian heritage.[5]

After Stalin's death in 1953, Akhmatova was gradually less censored by new leaders. She lived in a dacha in Komorovo, where young Russian poets could visit. Celebrated American poet Robert Frost also visited the dacha in 1962. After the release of new collections of her verse, she was allowed to visit Sicily and England to receive honors, traveling with her lifelong friend Lydia Korneievna Chukovskaya. When she met again with Sir Isaiah Berlin in Oxford in 1965, Akhmatova told him that Stalin had been personally enraged by the fact that she had allowed Berlin to visit her. Stalin's fury had unleashed the Cold War—and changed the history of mankind.[6]

Akhmatova has been called "one of the greatest Russian poets of the 20th-century, who became a legend in her own time as a poet and symbol of artistic integrity. Akhmatova's work is characterized by precision, clarity, and economy."[7] She died of heart failure on March 5, 1966.

Clive James wrote: "when a poet becomes better known than her poems, it usually means that she is being sacrificed, for extraneous reasons, on the altar of her own glory. In Akhmatova's case, the extraneous reasons were political."[8] It was only after the collapse of the Soviet Union that *Requiem*, her greatest cycle of poems, was published in her homeland on the hundredth anniversary of her birth.

AGATHA CHRISTIE (1890–1976)

In Torquay, England, best-selling author Agatha Christie was born as Agatha Mary Clarissa Miller. In their wealthy upper-middle-class family, she was the youngest of three children. Young Agatha was encouraged to write by her mother, who educated her at home. When she was sixteen, Agatha studied vocals and piano in Paris.

"I found myself making up stories and acting the different parts. There's nothing like boredom to make you write," she said later about her youth. "So by the time I was sixteen or seventeen, I'd written quite a number of short stories and one long, dreary novel. By the time I was twenty-one, I finished the first book of mine ever to be published."[9]

Her first attempts to become a published writer were not successful. On the advice of her mother, she consulted a neighbor and family friend, writer Eden Philpotts. Not only did Philpotts encourage as the best-selling novelist of all time, and the most translated author, with her works appearing in at least 103 languages.[10]

To honor her work as a writer, in 1956 Christie was appointed a Commander of the Order of the British Empire. In 1971, Christie was made a Dame Commander of the Order of the British Empire for her contribution to literature. She continued to write, in spite of failing health. Textual analysis of her books has led Canadian researchers to suggest that Alzheimer's disease or a similar dementia might have begun to affect Christie, because in her later books the vocabulary and sentence structure became simpler. Her final public appearance was in 1974, at the opening of a play based on *Murder on the Orient Express*. She died in 1976.

SIMONE DE BEAUVOIR (1908–1986)

The French writer Simone de Beauvoir was a feminist, influential social theorist, political activist, and existentialist philosopher. She was born January 9, 1908, in the 6th arrondissement of Paris in France. Her parents named her Simone Lucie Ernestine Marie Bertrand de Beauvoir. She was raised a Catholic in the closed society of proper bourgeois Paris.

"When I was a child, when I was an adolescent, books saved me from despair," de Beauvoir wrote in her book *The Woman Destroyed*. "That convinced me that culture was the highest of values."

When young Simone finished her early schooling, the opportunity to attend university was extended to women in France. Her mother worried that Simone would lose her faith, ignoring the fact that this had already occurred. At the Sorbonne, she studied philosophy, despite her father's objections that it was nothing but gibberish. Among her fellow students, she met Jean-Paul Sartre, and felt she was right to dream of being an intellectual and to associate with him. Though she was a young woman with no dowry, she now knew she had options other than marriage. She did not have to accept the expectations of a bourgeois life. Simone de Beauvoir became the ninth woman to receive a degree from the Sorbonne and began her life's work as a writer.

De Beauvoir wrote essays, biographies, and an autobiography as well as monographs on philosophy, politics, and social issues. Her novels gained more attention, including *The Mandarins* and *She Came to Stay*. Her most-read work was *The Second Sex*, an analysis of women's oppression, which has become a founding tract of contemporary feminism. Her writing has had a significant influence on feminist theory as well as on existentialism.

The relationship that de Beauvoir had with her partner Jean-Paul Sartre was lifelong, and unusual

BETTY FRIEDAN (1921–2006)

Betty Friedan was a suburban housewife who became a prominent activist for women's rights. Born Bettye Naomi Goldstein in Peoria, Illinois, she was the daughter of Harry and Miriam Goldstein. Her Jewish families came to America from Russia and Hungary. Her father owned a jewelry store, and when he fell ill, her mother wrote for the society page of a newspaper. Young Bettye noticed that her mother seemed much more satisfied working outside the home.

At the women-only Smith College, Bettye edited the newspaper, wrote political editorials—and dropped the final "e" from her name. She graduated summa cum laude in 1942. At the University of California, Berkeley, she trained with Erik Erikson to be a psychologist. Instead, she became a housewife and mother in the suburbs of New York. In 1947 she married Carl Friedan, a theater director, with whom she raised three children. To supplement the family income, she wrote freelance articles for women's magazines.

At her fifteen-year reunion, she surveyed her classmates from Smith, finding most of them to be dissatisfied suburban housewives, like her. She began a five-year research project, interviewing women across the United States and researching history, sociology, psychology, and economics. She charted

Betty Friedan's *The Feminine Mystique* struck a chord with American women in the 1960s and sowed the seeds of the second-wave feminist movement.

the metamorphosis of American middle-class women from the career-oriented independent New Woman of the 1920s and '30s to the housewife of the post-war years. Her research became her 1963 book *The Feminine Mystique*, one of the most influential books of the century.[14] In fact, it inspired the women's movement of the 1960s and '70s.

In 1971, Friedan became a cofounder and leader for the National Organization for Women, working to improve women's rights. She also helped found and lead other women's groups, which were integral in helping to change outdated laws that put women at a disadvantage. The women's movement included those who criticized Friedan for focusing on issues of interest primarily to women who were white, middle-class, educated, and heterosexual. Other radicals in the feminist movement disapproved that Friedan worked with men. But over time, Friedan was a mainstream balance for other leaders' more radical attitudes, and she gained solidarity with people of marginalized gender and orientation.

Friedan went on to write six more books, to teach at New York University and the University of Southern California, and to lecture at women's conferences worldwide. For the rest of her life, she was active in politics and advocacy groups. She died in 2006 of congestive heart failure. Her obituary noted that she was "famously abrasive," as well as "thin-skinned and imperious, subject to screaming fits of temperament."[15] Some of her papers are held in the Schlesinger Library at Radcliffe Institute.

CHAPTER SIX

WOMEN WRITERS WHO SPEAK TO TODAY

In the twenty-first century, it is no longer a social convention that a woman writer must have a male family member to be her agent to interact with her publisher. Nor is it necessary for a writer who is a married woman to have her husband cosign any contracts she makes. In Western countries, feminist movements have succeeded in advocating for laws to be written recognizing the human rights of women. More people can read and write now than ever before, and people can self-publish their own writing on the Internet, renting time on a computer for the price of a cheap meal. Unfortunately, some women whose writing appears on the Internet are subjected to virulent verbal abuse and death threats from men who condemn them for expressing opinions. Some of the women profiled in this chapter were born before those changes, and others lived while those social rules were changing.

prosperous businessman who had been a lieutenant in the German army during the First World War. In their quiet neighborhood, a religiously diverse area in a suburb of Frankfurt, the Frank family were typical of upper-middle-class German Jews.

As the German economy struggled through the Great Depression, Otto Frank feared for his family when storm troopers marched the streets. When Hitler came to power in 1933, the Frank family moved to Amsterdam. They were relieved to be free from anti-Semitism, and Otto Frank "became managing director of the Dutch Opekta Company which manufactures products used in making jam," as Anne later wrote in her diary.[4]

Young Anne began attending Amsterdam's Sixth Montessori School in 1934, where she was a bright and inquisitive student. She had many friends, including Dutch and Germans, Jews and Christians. Their lives began to change when the Nazis occupied the Netherlands. The Franks applied to emigrate to England and to America, but were turned down.[5]

In October 1940, anti-Jewish measures were imposed by the Nazis. Jews were forbidden from owning a business, and a strict curfew was set on their movements. They were required to wear a yellow Star of David on their clothing. Anne and her sister Margot were forced to transfer to a segregated Jewish school. Their father signed control of his company over to two of his Christian associates.

For Anne's thirteenth birthday, her parents gave her a diary with a red-checkered cover. That day she wrote her first entry, addressing it to an imaginary friend she named Kitty. The idea of having someone to confide in gave her hope for comfort and support. Another attempt to emigrate to America was refused.

Anne Frank's diary, written while her family hid from the Nazis, is an important firsthand account of the Holocaust.

Only weeks later, her sister was summoned to report to a Nazi work camp in Germany. The Frank family went into hiding the next day, in unused rooms at the back of the Dutch Opekta Company building. With them were Otto Frank's business partner, with his wife and son. Food and information about current events was brought to them by Otto's Christian employees. A dentist friend joined them in hiding that fall.

During the two years these eight Jewish people remained in hiding, they lived very quietly and never went outside. Deprived of her studies and social life, Anne wrote in her diary about her experiences and her wishes for the future. Some entries show the despair she felt after days of confinement, but writing helped her keep her sanity and good spirits.

Betrayed by an anonymous tip to the Nazis, the families were discovered and arrested on August 4, 1944. Shipped first by train to a concentration camp in northeastern Netherlands, they were transferred to Poland. At Auschwitz death camp, the men and women were separated.

After months of hard labor, Anne and Margot were transferred to Bergen-Belsen concentration camp. Their mother was kept at Auschwitz and died that winter. In Bergen-Belsen, there was poor sanitation and little food. Anne and Margot were not the only ones to become ill from typhus. The sisters died within a day of each other in March 1945, only a few weeks before the camp was liberated by British soldiers. One of over a million Jewish children who died in the Holocaust, Anne was only fifteen years old.

Her father survived, returning to Amsterdam in July 1945, where he learned of his daughters' deaths from friends they had made. Among the Frank family possessions saved by a Dutch employee was Anne's diary. When he read it, Otto Frank was deeply impressed by her thoughts and feelings. He chose selections from Anne's diary to be published as a book in 1947. *The Diary of a Young Girl*, as it is called in English, has been read by millions of people, translated into sixty-seven languages, and adapted for stage and film. It is perhaps the most widely read firsthand account of the experience of Jews during the Holocaust. The diary is read and respected not only because of the events Anne described but because she is a gifted storyteller. Her spirit remains strong even through horrific conditions.

TONI MORRISON (1931–)

Toni Morrison was named Chloe Anthony Wofford at birth in Lorain, Ohio, the second oldest of four children. George Wofford, her father, was a welder by trade, and held several jobs at once to support the family. Her mother, Ramah, was a domestic worker. Both parents helped their children to love reading, music, and folklore. Their home was in an integrated neighborhood, and as a child, young Toni was not fully aware of racial divisions until she was a teenager. "When I was in first grade, nobody thought I was inferior," she later said in an interview. "I was the only black in the class and the only child who could read."[6] She listened to the radio as a child, imagining things she heard. Young Toni studied Latin and English Literature at Lorain High School, graduating with honors in 1949.

At Howard University, she majored in English with a minor in Classics. For her master's degree at Cornell University, she wrote on the works of Virginia Woolf and William Faulkner. At Texas Southern University, she taught English literature.

Among other awards, Toni Morrison's work has earned her the Nobel, the Pulitzer, and the Presidential Medal of Honor.

When she returned to Howard University in 1957 to teach, she met architect Harold Morrison. They married in 1958. After their first son was born, Toni Morrison became part of a group of writers meeting on campus. The short story she started working on with them became a novel.

After spending the summer of 1963 traveling with her family in Europe, Morrison returned to the United States with her son, but her husband had decided he would return to his birthplace, Jamaica. Pregnant with their second child, Morrison moved back to Ohio to live with her family while her son was born. In 1965, she found work as a senior editor with a textbook publisher, and so she moved to Syracuse, New York, with her sons. Later, Morrison was hired by Random House to edit works by popular and successful authors.

The Bluest Eye was Morrison's first novel, published in 1970. Like many of her books, it explores the African American experience. "I wrote the first book because I wanted to read it," Morrison later said. "I thought that kind of book, with that subject—those most vulnerable, most undescribed, not-taken-seriously little black girls—had never existed seriously in literature. No one had ever written about them except as props."[7]

Her early works received accolades and moderately good sales. As a rising literary star, Morrison woke early to write while working full-time, and was appointed to the National Council on the Arts from 1980–87. She became a professor at Princeton University in 1989, establishing a special workshop for writers and performers. Her books continued to sell widely and to excite critics and reviewers. In 1993, she became the first African American woman to be awarded the Nobel Prize in Literature. She has gone on to write books for children, plays, and song lyrics, including the libretto for *Margaret Garner*, an American opera on the tragedy of slavery. "In all her projects," wrote one critic, "her words are at once incisive as a knife and poignant as a lullaby, weaving mesmerizing narratives that probe the complexities of the African-American experience."[8]

Now retired from Princeton, Morrison is a champion for the arts, speaking and writing on issues of free speech and censorship. She has survived the death of one of her sons. In her eighties, she worked on an opera based on *Othello*, and she continues to write novels exploring different eras.

MARGARET ATWOOD (1939–)

Margaret Eleanor Atwood was born in Ottawa, Ontario, Canada, on November 18, 1939. Her parents were originally from Nova Scotia, and Margaret (known as Peggy in her youth) was the second of their three children. Her mother, Margaret Dorothy Killam, was a dietician and a nutritionist. Carl Atwood, her father, was a forest entomologist, and for much of her childhood his work took the family into the forests of Ontario every spring till fall, with baby Peggy in a back-pack at first.[9] The children were given lessons by their mother each morning, and invented their own imaginative play. When young Peggy was seven, her family moved to Toronto. While at high school, she resolved to become a writer.

Atwood attended the University of Toronto, majoring in English, with minors in Philosophy and French. In 1961, she received her BA with honors, and went on to get her master's degree from Radcliffe College in Massachusetts, in 1962. She did two two-year periods of study at Harvard for her PhD, but did not finish.

Like many poets, Margaret Atwood had to self-publish her first collection of poems, *Double Persephone*, in 1961. Her second book, *The Circle Game*, was published by Cranbrook Academy of Art and won Canada's governor general's award for poetry in 1964. Since then, she has written over fifteen collections of her poetry, and individual poems have appeared in numerous magazines and journals.

Atwood married writer Jim Polk in 1967, but they drifted apart and separated after a few years. In 1969 Atwood received good reviews for her first novel, *The Edible Woman*, the story of a woman who feels as if she is being eaten. As her second novel, *Surfacing*, was launched in 1972, Atwood married writer

Few writers today are as respected for a robust and varied body of work as Margaret Atwood.

Graeme Gibson. She moved to the small town of Alliston, Ontario, with Gibson and his two young sons. In 1976, they had a daughter.

Critics, academics, and readers alike regard Margaret Atwood as "one of the most noteworthy writers of our time."[10] Many of her novels and collections of her stories have won multiple international awards. Her many nonfiction works have considerable influence in Canadian literature. Atwood's short works include book reviews, literary criticism, studies, political essays, autobiographical essays, eulogies, and ecological writings; some are collected into ten books. She also writes newspaper and magazine stories and other journalism. She wrote eight books for children, the first of which she illustrated in two-color drawings. As well, Atwood invented the LongPen and developed associated technologies to allow documents to be written remotely, including books to be signed by an author.[11] "In novels such as *Oryx and Crake* and *The Handmaid's Tale*, Ms Atwood has demonstrated that she has few equals when it comes to imagining the transformative powers of technology on humanity,"[12] wrote one reviewer. Atwood has said at writer's conventions: "Don't speak so softly that you can't be heard, nor so loudly that you're deafening."

J. K. ROWLING (1965–)

In five years of dedicated writing, a single mother on state benefits went from unpublished to the most successful writer of books for young people. On July 31, 1965, Joanne Rowling was born in Yate, England, daughter of Anne Rowling, a science technician, and Peter James Rowling, an aircraft engineer. After the age of nine, young Joanne moved with her family to Chepstow, Gwent. She and her younger sister Di attended Saint Michael's Primary School, and in their teens Wyedean Comprehensive school.

At Exeter University, Rowling studied French and Classics. After graduating in 1986, she moved to London and worked at several jobs, including as a researcher and bilingual secretary at Amnesty International. She began the manuscript that was to become her first book in her Harry Potter series in 1990, while waiting for a delayed train on the run from Manchester to London King's Cross. During the next five years, she outlined the plots for the series and began writing the first novel.

With a move to Porto, Portugal, Rowling wrote in her spare time from a job as an English language teacher. In 1992, she married a Portuguese TV producer and together they had a daughter. The couple separated in 1993.

After her marriage broke up, Rowling and her baby daughter moved to Edinburgh, Scotland, and lived in a tiny apartment. It was hard to make ends meet on welfare, but Rowling budgeted carefully. Her mother had died of multiple sclerosis, and depression was a problem for her. While her baby slept beside her, Rowling took time in coffee shops to write. She said later of this time, "I think I wanted to write because words were always my safe place."[13]

When she sent her manuscript for *Harry Potter and the Philosopher's Stone* to a publisher, success was not automatic. "I pinned my first rejection letter to my kitchen wall because it gave me something in common with all my fave writers!" she wrote later on Twitter.[14] The manuscript was turned down by many publishers, one after another, but Rowling kept trying. "I wasn't going to give up until every

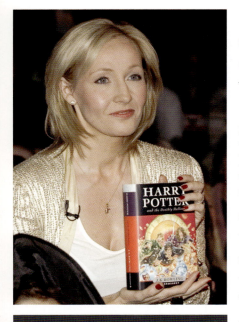

J. K. Rowling's first novel, *Harry Potter and the Philosopher's Stone*, was rejected twelve times before she found a publisher.

single publisher turned me down, but I often feared that would happen."[15]

It was 1997 before her first book was published, by Bloomsbury Children's Books. Bloomsbury editor Barry Cunningham had asked his eight-year-old daughter to read the first chapter. When she demanded the rest, he decided to publish Rowling's book. The publisher felt that the target audience of young boys would not be interested in a book written by a woman, so they substituted her first name with initials. Joanne Rowling had no middle name, so she used K for Kathleen, which was her paternal grandmother's name. Cunningham advised Rowling to get a day job, as it is hard to earn a living as an author of children's books, but she was lucky enough to get a grant of £8000 from the Scottish Arts Council to write a sequel.

With the release in July 1998 of the second book in the series, sales momentum began to increase for each book Rowling wrote. The seventh book in the series sold eleven million copies in the UK alone on its first day of sales in July 2007, breaking the sixth book's record as the fastest-selling book of all time. Her Harry Potter books have become the best-selling series of books in history, and they have been the basis for the second-highest grossing film series; for the films, Rowling maintained creative control. The series has been translated into sixty-five languages.

In 2007, Forbes announced that Rowling was the first-ever author to become a billionaire, but Rowling disputed that statistic at the time. Income continues to flow in from her Harry Potter books and the films and merchandise based on them. As a dedicated philanthropist, Rowling did not retain this extraordinary personal wealth for long. She founded Lumos, a charity that works to transform the lives of disadvantaged children, and she gives a substantial portion of her wealth to support charitable causes through her charitable trust Volant, named after her mother's maiden name.

Following her wildly successful Harry Potter series, Rowling is writing some related works as well as novels for adults. The novels were sent to publishers under a pseudonym, and were eventually published, having good sales even before she was revealed as the author.[16] A pen name she uses is Robert Galbraith, a male name in order to be different from herself. She posted on Twitter about sending manuscripts to be considered: "Yes, the publisher who first turned down Harry also sent @ Rgalbraith his rudest rejection (by email)!"[17]

When asked by a fan how to perservere in the face of failure, Rowling turned to her own experience: "I had nothing to lose and sometimes that makes you brave enough to try."[18] When Rowling first began writing, she was a working single mother, with little support and encouragement. She wrote the first Harry Potter book using a paper notebook and an old manual typewriter rather than an expensive computer.

Rowling has received numerous awards and honorary degrees, as well as an Order of the British Empire for services to children's literature. She lives in Edinburgh, Scotland, with her second husband, Neil Michael Murray, an anesthetist, and their three children.

CONCLUSION

Now, in the twenty-first century, there are more women writers than ever before, particularly for works published in English. Some lead isolated private lives, while others are research scientists and academics. The careers of women writers who are active in public life range widely, from embedded journalists attached to military units in combat zones to songwriters and performers.

Even so, there is still an ongoing prejudice against

women writers. On average, women authors are paid a lower advance on book contracts than men. Most published books are written by men, even though romance writers are nearly all women, and romance novels make up about half of all paperback books sold. Men wrote 83 percent of books reviewed by the *New York Times* in 2011.[19] The publishing, television, film, and gaming industries are all dominated by men and by white people of European descent.[20]

Only in the genre of science fiction and fantasy books, itself marginalized from mainstream literature, are female writers and writers of color published to any extent remotely similar to their numbers in the population at large. Even J. K. Rowling, the first writer to become a billionaire from book sales, used her initials because her publisher did not want to associate a woman's name with her book. But as modern social media forums spread with minimal censorship by way of the Internet, people from many countries and cultures are discovering the powerful communication of writing, as it has been enjoyed since the Stone Age.

CHAPTER NOTES

INTRODUCTION

1. Genevieve von Petzinger, "Geometric Signs: a New Understanding," *The Bradshaw Foundation*, March 1, 2016, http://www.bradshawfoundation.com/geometric_signs/.
2. Simone de Beauvoir, Quoted by Leigh Turner, "Simone de Beauvoir's Got Your Number, Slim," *Foreign & Commonwealth Office*, March 30, 2016, http://blogs.fco.gov.uk/leighturner/2013/03/08/high-heels-ambassadors-and-simone-de-beauvoir/.

CHAPTER 1. WOMEN WRITING BEFORE THE CHRISTIAN ERA

1. "Sheba," *Encyclopedia of World Biography*, February 26, 2016, http://www.encyclopedia.com/topic/Queen_of_Sheba.aspx.
2. Miguel F. Brooks, translator, Kebra Negast (Trenton, NJ: The Red Sea Press, 1996).
3. "Song of Solomon 1:5," *King James Bible online*, February 26, 2016, https://www.kingjamesbibleonline.org/Song-of-Solomon-1-5/.
4. Bernard Suler, "Alchemy," *Encyclopedia Judaica*, March 1, 2016, http://www.jewishvirtuallibrary.org/jsource/judaica/ejud_0002_0001_0_00704.html.
5. Ibrahim Omer, "Evidence Mounts of Ancient Jewish Roots of Beta Israel Ethiopian Jewry," *Genetic Literacy Project*, June 16, 2015, https://www.geneticliteracyproject.org/2015/06/16/

evidence-mounts-of-ancient-jewish-roots-of-beta-israel-ethiopian-jewry/.

6. Nicholas Clapp, *Sheba: Through the Desert in Search of the Legendary Queen*, (New York: Houghton Mifflin, 2001).

7. Marjorie Bingham, "Ten Essential Women for a World History Class," *World History Connected*, March 10, 2016,http://worldhistoryconnected. press.illinois.edu/4.3/bingham.html.

8. Daniel Mendelson, "Girl, Interrupted. Who was Sappho?" *The New Yorker*, March 16, 2015, http://www.newyorker.com/magazine/2015/03/16/girl-interrupted.

9. Alix North, "Sappho," *Isle of Lesbos*, Updated 2007, February 27, 2016, http://www.sappho.com/poetry/sappho.html.

10. Writer 873, "Aspasia: Influential Concubine to Pericles," *Ancient History Encyclopedia* website, February 26, 2016, http://www.ancient.eu/article/73/.

11. James Grout, "Hetaira," *Encyclopedia Romana* website, University of Chicago, Updated May 4, 2015, March 4, 2016, http://penelope.uchicago.edu/-grout/encyclopaedia_romana/greece/hetairai/hetairai.html.

12. Madeleine Henry, *Prisoner of History: Aspasia of Miletus and her Biographical Tradition* (New York: Oxford University Press, 1995), p. 128.

13. Socrates Scholaticus, *Ecclesiastical History*

website, March 6, 2016, http://cosmopolis.com/alexandria/hypatia-bio-socrates.html.

14. Brian Haughton, "What Happened to the Great Library of Alexandria?" *Ancient History* website, February 1, 2011, http://www.ancient.eu/article/207/.

15. Michael A. B. Deakin, *Hypatia of Alexandria: Mathematician and Martyr* (Amherst, NY: Prometheus Books, 2007).

16. Christine Walsh, *The Cult of St. Katherine of Alexandria in Early Medieval Europe* (New York: Routledge, 2007), p. 10.

17. *Ecclesiastical History* website.

18. "Catalog listing: Hypatia of Alexandria," *Prometheus Books* website, March 6, 2016. http://www.prometheusbooks.com/index.php?main_page=product_info&cPath=29_206&products_id=1754.

CHAPTER 2. WOMEN WRITERS IN THE MIDDLE AGES

1. Myriam Francois-Cerrah, "The Truth About Muhammad and Aisha," *The Guardian*, Updated September 17, 2012, http://www.theguardian.com/commentisfree/belief/2012/sep/17/muhammad-aisha-truth.

2. D. A. Spellberg, *Politics, Gender, and the Islamic Past: the Legacy of A'isha bint Abi Bakr* (New York:

Columbia University Press, 1994), p. 4.

3. Marjorie Bingham, "Ten Essential Women for a World History Class," World History Connected, March 10, 2016,http://worldhis-toryconnected.press.illinois.edu/4.3/bingham.html.

4. Tanu Wakefield, "Stanford Poetry Scholar Offers New Perspective on China's Most Revered Female Poet," *Stanford News*, March 10, 2016, http://news.stanford.edu/news/2014/july/qingzhao-chinese-poet-071614.html.

5. Victor H. Mair, editor, Jiaosheng Wang, *The Complete Ci-poems of Li Qingzhao: A New English Translation*, Sino-Platonic Papers (Philadelphia, PA: University of Pennsylvania, 1989),http://sino-platonic.org/complete/spp013_li_qing-zhao.pdf.

6. James E. Kiefer, "Hildegard of Bingen, Visionary," *Biographical Sketches of Memorable Christians of the Past*, March 18, 2016, http://justus.anglican.org/resources/bio/247.html.

7. Tejvan Pettinger, "Biography of Mirabai," *Biography Online*, Last updated August 3 2014, March 2, 2016, http://www.biographyonline.net/spiritual/mirabai.html.

8. "Mirabai," *Women in World History*, Updated 2016, March 5, 2016, http://www.womenin-worldhistory.com/heroine12.html.

CHAPTER 3. WOMEN WRITING DURING THE ENLIGHTENMENT

1. Charlotte Gordon, *Romantic Outlaws: the Extraordinary Lives of Mary Wollstonecraft and Her Daughter Mary Shelley* (New York: Random House, 2015), p. xvii.

2. Ibid.

3. Renee Warren, "Jane Austen, Biography," Jane Austen website, Updated 2016, March 30, 2016, http://www.janeausten.org/jane-austen-biography.asp.

4. Z. Cope, "Jane Austen's Last Illness," *British Medical Journal* 2, no. 5402 (1964): 182–3 PMID: 14150900.

5. Sarah Milligan, "Sonnets and the Sickroom: The Invalid Persona in Elizabeth Barrett Browning's Sonnets from the Portuguese," MA essay, University of Victoria, 2012.

6. Jennifer Kingma Wall, "Love and Marriage: How Biographical Interpretation Affected the Reception of Elizabeth Barrett Browning's Sonnets from the Portuguese (1850)," Victorian Web, May 4, 2005, http://www.victorianweb.org/authors/ebb/wall1.html (November 12, 2012).

7. "Harriet Beecher Stowe's Life," *Harriet Beecher Stowe Center*, March 10, 2016, https://www.harrietbeecherstowecenter.org/hbs/.

8. Lorna Sage, Germaine Greer, and Elaine Showater, "Stowe, Harriet (Elizabeth) Beecher,"

The Cambridge Guide to Women's Writing in English (Cambridge, UK: Cambridge University Press, 1999), p. 605.

9. "Harriet Beecher Stowe's Life," *Harriet Beecher Stowe Center*, March 10, 2016, https://www.harrietbeecherstowecenter.org/hbs/.

CHAPTER 4. WOMEN WRITERS IN THE INDUSTRIAL REVOLUTION

1. Eleanor Wachtel, "Claire Harman on the Passions and Frustrations of Charlotte Brontë," *Writers and Company, CBC Radio One*, Broadcast Sunday, March 13, 2016, http://www.cbc.ca/radio/writersandcompany/claire-harman-on-the-passions-and-frustrations-of-charlotte-bront%C3%AB-1.3483242.

2. Deborah Lutz, *The Brontë Cabinet: Three Lives in Nine Objects* (New York: W. W. Norton, 2015).

3. Wachtel, ibid.

4. Gordon S. Height, "George Eliot, British author," *Encyclopaedia Britannica, Biography*. March 22, 2016, http://www.britannica.com/biography/George-Eliot.

5. Rebecca Mead, "George Eliot's Ugly Beauty," *The New Yorker*, September 19, 2013, http://www.newyorker.com/books/page-turner/george-eliots-ugly-beauty.

6. Ibid.

7. Ibid.

8. George Eliot's Ugly Beauty.

9. Paula Johanson, "Emily Dickinson," *Love Poetry: How Do I Love Thee?* (New York: Enslow Publishing, 2014).

10. Norman Foerster, "Emily Dickinson," Ward & Trent, et al., *The Cambridge History of English and American Literature* (New York: G. P. Putnam's Sons, 1907–1921; New York: Bartleby.com, 2000).

11. Roland Hagenbuchle, "Sumptuous—Despair: The Function of Desire in Emily Dickinson's Poetry," *The Emily Dickinson Journal*, vol. 5, no. 2: Fall 1996, pp. 1–9, March 10, 2016, http://muse.jhu.edu/journals/edj/summary/v005/5.2.hagenbuchle.html.

12. Sumptuous—Despair.

13. Emily Dickinson, Ward & Trent.

14. Lorna Sage, Germaine Greer, and Elaine Showater, "Alcott, Louisa May," *The Cambridge Guide to Women Writing in English* (Cambridge, UK: Cambridge University Press, 1999), p. 8.

15. Jan Turnquist, "Louisa May Alcott," *Louisa May Alcott Memorial Association*, Updated 2004, March 10, 2016, http://www.louisamayalcott.org/louisamaytext.html.

16. "Johnson Family Tree," *Chiefswood National Historic Site*, (accessed 27 May 2011), Quoted by Betty Keller, *Pauline: A Biography of Pauline* (Halifax, NS: Formac Publishing, 1981).

17. Charlotte Gray, *Flint & Feather: The Life and Times of E. Pauline Johnson, Tekahionwake* (Toronto, ON: HarperCollins, 2002).

18. "Margaret Atwood's Opera Debut, Pauline Opens in Vancouver," *CBC News* website, March 2, 2016, http://www.cbc.ca/news/arts/margaret-atwood-s-opera-debut-pauline-opens-in-vancouver-1.2652605.

19. Ibid.

CHAPTER 5. WOMEN WRITING IN THE TWENTIETH CENTURY

1. S. N. Clarke, "Virginia Woolf: A Short Biography," *Virginia Woolf Society of Great Britain*, March 2, 2016, http://www.virginiawoolfsociety.co.uk/vw_res.biography.htm.

2. Maxwell Bennett, *Virginia Woolf and Neuropsychiatry* (London: Springer, 2013), p. 3.

3. Hermione Lee, *Virginia Woolf* (New York: Vintage, 1998), p. 4.

4. Paula Johanson, "Anna Akhmatova," *World Poetry: Evidence of Life* (New York: Enslow Publishing, 2010).

5. Clive James, "Anna Akhmatova," *Slate.com*, March 1, 2016, http://www.slate.com/articles/news_and_politics/clives_lives/2007/02/anna_akhmatova.html.

6. Petri Liukkonen, "Anna Akhmatova," *Books and*

Writers website December 15, 2008, http://www.kirjasto.sci.fi/aakhma.htm.

7. Anna Akhmatova.

8. Anna Akhmatova.

9. "Agatha Christie," *Biography.com*, March 1 2016, http://www.biography.com/people/agatha-christie-9247405#background.

10. Norris McWhirter and Ross McWhirter, Guinness Book of World Records, 11th US Edition (New York: Bantam Books, 1976), p. 704.

11. "Simone de Beauvoir." *Encyclopedia Britannica*, Updated 2016, March 19, 2016, http://www.britannica.com/biography/Simone-de-Beauvoir.

12. Susan J. Brison, "Beauvoir and Feminism: Interview and Reflections," *The Cambridge Companion to Simone de Beauvoir*, edited by Claudia Card (Cambridge, UK: Cambridge University Press), p. 202.

13. Ibid.

14. "Betty Friedan," National Women's History Museum, March 11, 2016, https://www.nwhm.org/education-resources/biography/biographies/betty-friedan/.

15. Margaret Fox, "Betty Friedan, Who Ignited Cause in 'Feminine Mystique,' Dies at 85," *New York Times*, March 10, 2016,http://www.nytimes.com/2006/02/05/national/05friedan.html?pagewanted=all&_r=0.

CHAPTER 6. WOMEN WRITERS WHO SPEAK TO TODAY

1. "Maya Angelou Biography," *Academy of Achievement*, Updated May 28, 2014, March 3, 2016, http://www.achievement.org/autodoc/page/angobio-1.

2. Margalit Fox, "Maya Angelou: Lyrical Witness of the Jim Crow South, Dies at 86," *New York Times*, March 29, 2016, http://www.nytimes.com/2014/05/29/arts/maya-angelou-lyrical-witness-of-the-jim-crow-south-dies-at-86.html?_r=0.

3. "Biography," Caged Bird Legacy, Updated 2016, March 2, 2016, http://www.mayaangelou.com/biography/;http://www.achievement.org/autodoc/page/angobio-1.

4. "Anne Frank Biography," *Biography.com*, March 2, 2016,http://www.biography.com/people/anne-frank-9300892#early-life.

5. "The Story of Anne Frank in Brief," *Anne Frank*, March 1, 2016, http://www.annefrank.org/en/Anne-Frank/Anne-Franks-history-in-brief/.

6. "Toni Morrison Biography," *Biography.com*, Updated 2016, March 4, 2016, http://www.biography.com/people/toni-morrison-9415590.

7. Rebecca Gross, with Toni Morrison, "Write, Erase, Do It Over: On Failure, Risk and Writing Outside Yourself," *American Theatre*, March 3, 2016, http://www.americantheatre.

org/2015/03/10/write-erase-do-it-over-on-fail-ure-risk-and-writing-outside-yourself/.

8. Ibid.

9. Robert Potts, "Light in the Wilderness," *The Guardian*, March 16, 2016, http://www.theguardian.com/books/2003/apr/26/fiction.margaretatwood.

10. Annina Jokinen, "Margaret Atwood," *Luminarium: Anthology of English Literature*, Updated 2007, March 15, 2016, http://www.luminarium.org/contemporary/atwood/atwood.htm.

11. Oliver Burkeman, "Atwood Sign of the Times Draws Blank," *The Guardian*, March 6, 2016, http://www.theguardian.com/world/2006/mar/06/topstories3.books.

12. Margaret Atwood, *Luminarium*.

13. J. K. Rowling, Twitter.com, March 15, 2016, https://twitter.com/jk_rowling/status/709739338612002817.

14. J. K. Rowling, Twitter.com, March 25, 2016, https://twitter.com/jk_rowling/status/713287517911560192.

15. J. K. Rowling, Twitter.com, March 25, 2016, https://twitter.com/jk_rowling/status/713292055284424704.

16. Hannah Furness, "JK Rowling Reveals Cringe-worthy Rejection Letter Telling Her to Join Writing Class," *The Telegraph*, March 25, 2016, http://www.telegraph.co.uk/news/celebritynews/12204161/

JK-Rowling-reveals-cringe-worthy-rejection-letter-teaching-grandmother-to-suck-eggs.html.

17. J. K. Rowling, Twitter.com, March 25, 2016, https://twitter.com/jk_rowling/status/713301256811507712.

18. J. K. Rowling, Twitter.com, March 25, 2016, https://twitter.com/jk_rowling/status/713301256811507712.

19. Benedict Page, "Research Shows Male Writers Still Dominate Books World," *The Guardian.com*, February 4, 2011, http://www.theguardian.com/books/2011/feb/04/research-male-writers-dominate-books-world.

20. Roxane Gay, "Where Things Stand," *The Rumpus*, June 6, 2012, http://therumpus.net/2012/06/where-things-stand/, and Hess, Amanda, "Why 88% of books reviewed by The New York Times are written by white authors," *Poynter*, June 11, 2012, http://www.poynter.org/2012/why-88-of-books-reviewed-by-the-new-york-times-are-written-by-white-authors/176705/.

GLOSSARY

ascetic Person who lives with minimal comforts to focus on matters of the mind or religion.

bluestocking An educated intellectual.

charisma Having the characteristics of being very interesting, appealing, and believable.

enjambment The continuation of a sentence over a line break in poetry.

juvenilia The writing an author did in childhood or as a student, whether published or unpublished.

Neoplatonism Philosophy in which philosophers discussed the origin of the human soul and how the soul may return to the eternal Divine.

patron A person who supports a writer or an artist by contributing money and encouragement, formally or informally.

Platonism The belief that physical objects are impermanent representations of unchanging ideas, and that those ideas alone give true knowledge as they are known by the mind.

potboiler An inferior work of fiction printed on cheap paper, usually formulaic and undemanding.

salon A room in which learned people gather for discussions on literary matters and science.

samizdat A Russian word for amateur publications created and circulated unofficially, when government approval was needed for any published work.

volta Dramatic emotional turn in poetry.

FURTHER READING

BOOKS

Eger, Elizabeth. *Bluestockings: Women of Reason from Enlightenment to Romanticism*. London: Palgrave Macmillan, 2010.

Gordon, Charlotte. *Romantic Outlaws: The Extraordinary Lives of Mary Wollstonecraft and Her Daughter Mary Shelley*. New York, NY: Random House, 2015.

Harman, Claire. *Charlotte Brontë: A Fiery Heart*. Toronto, ON: Knopf Canada, 2016.

Hoeveler, Diane Long, and Deborah Denenholz Morse. *A Companion to the Brontës*. Toronto, ON: Wiley-Blackwell, 2016.

Johnson, E. Pauline (Tekahionwake). *Flint and Feather: Collected Verse*. Leopold Classic Library, 2015.

Lee, Edmund. *Dorothy Wordsworth: The Story of a Sister's Love*. London: FB &c Ltd., 2015.

Lutz, Deborah. *The Brontë Cabinet: Three Lives in Nine Objects*. New York, NY: W. W. Norton, 2015.

Wollstonecraft, Mary. *A Vindication of the Rights of Woman*. Wollstonecraft Books, 2013.

WEBSITES

Canadian Women Poets
www.brocku.ca/canadianwomenpoets/
Explore the works, criticisms, lives, and awards
of Canada's most prominent female poets.

The Literature Network
www.online-literature.com
This searchable database contains more than
3,500 complete books and more than 4,400
short stories and poems by more than 260
authors

Luminarium: Anthology of English Literature
www.luminarium.org
This website provides the works, quotations,
essays, portraits, and biographies of English
authors from the Middle Ages, Renaissance,
Seventeenth Century, and Restoration.

Victorian Women Writers Project
webapp1.dlib.indiana.edu/vwwp/welcome.do
Discover the lives and works of lesser-known
women writers of the Victorian Era.

INDEX